Praise for How to Work a Room

Some people would rather kiss a snake than go to a cocktail party. This book is for you.

—Seth Godin, author of *Permission Marketing* and *Unleashing the Ideavirus*

This book gives you the game plan to tackle any group situations.

—John Ralston, professional speaker and former coach, Denver Broncos

I cannot understand how anyone can network until they have read this book! It is an essential career tool.

—Marilyn Moats Kennedy, author of *The Career Strategist*

There are no limp handshakes . . . for Susan RoAne. She charges into a room of strangers . . . and shares with crowds the roadblocks, remedies and responsibilities of business mingling.

—*Fresno Bee*

The ability to connect with colleagues, clients, and coworkers is essential for success. Susan RoAne's revised classic will guide you through any room, whether it's a roomful of strangers or associates.

—Connie Glaser, author of *When Money Isn't Enough*

Ever dreaded entering a roomful of strangers? Ever tried to walk across a room to introduce yourself to someone special but found your legs had turned to stone? Ever tried to be witty but discovered your brain just turned to mush? If any or all these things have happened to you, then buy this clever, informative and accessible book by Susan RoAne, the best conversationalist I know.

—Robert Spector, author of *Amazon.com: Get Big Fast*

How to Work a Room is a classic! No adult could be armed for life without it! Susan RoAne provides insights into interpersonal excellence and savvy social etiquette that they don't teach you in school! Unless you plan to survive on an island . . . by yourself—BUY THIS BOOK.

—D.

Susan RoAne (aka, "The Mingling Maven") has done it again! RoAne applies her sage advice, engaging wit, and personal charm, along with her empathy and support, to help others understand how to deal skillfully and compassionately with many everyday social situations that can serve as roadblocks to personal growth and professional development. Like the *Wizard of Oz,* her words will provide courage to the timid, confidence to the unsure, and knowledge to the misinformed about how to engage others in a manner characterized by style and comfort. Her extensive use of examples and specific recommendations for dealing with difficult social situations experienced by all of us in a variety of everyday settings, ranging from the boardroom to the boardwalk, from one's professional network to one's personal neighborhood, and from the use of cell phones to chat rooms, will inspire others to show their true personal strengths, without having to show off. A "must-read book" for those of us who want to enhance our most unique human quality—the ability to converse, connect, and embrace others locally and globally. In my view, the subtitle says it all: "The Ultimate Guide to Savvy Socializing In-Person and On-Line."

—Dr. Bernardo J. Carducci, Director of the Indiana University Southeast Shyness Research Institute, Fellow of the American Psychological Association, and author of *Shyness: A Bold New Approach*

HOW
TO
WORK
A ROOM

HOW
TO
WORK
A ROOM

THE ULTIMATE GUIDE TO
SAVVY SOCIALIZING
IN PERSON AND ONLINE

SUSAN RoAne

[handwritten inscription:]

12/11/0

Dear Dr.
Carucci:
Thank you so
much for your
wonderful endorsement
I hope you and I
get to meet at some
time ... maybe
on Oprah!

Best,
Susan RoAne

Quill
A HarperResource Book
An Imprint of HarperCollinsPublishers

HarperCollins books may be purchased for educational, business, or sales promotional use. For information, please write to: Special Markets Department, HarperCollins Publishers Inc., 10 East 53rd Street, New York, New York 10022.

HarperCollins edition

Designed by Nancy Singer Olaguera

Library of Congress Cataloging-In-Publication Data

RoAne, Susan 1945-
    How to work a room: the ultimate guide to savvy socializing in person and online / Susan RoAne.—HarperCollins ed.
        p. cm.
    Includes bibliographical references.
    ISBN 0-06-095785-9 (alk. paper)
        1. Business etiquette. 2. Business entertaining. 3. Public relations. 4. Interpersonal relations. I. Title.
    HF5387.R617 2000
    650.1'3—dc21

                                                            00-040948

00 01 02 03 04 ❖RRD 10 0 9 7 6 5 4 3 2 1

This book is rededicated IN MEMORIAM to the spirit of three special people:

To Ida Cohen, my grandmother, who imparted her wisdom, and whose homemade chicken soup was our soul food.

To Ida B. Harvey, my "assistant mother," who taught me that "beauty is only skin deep, but ugly . . . is to the bone."

To Sally Livingston, my "femtor"—female mentor—who was a guiding spirit, role model and cheerleader.

And to those whose words of wisdom, kindness and support echo eternally.

CONTENTS

The Business Kiss

Another "Touchy" Subject

RoAne's Reminders

1. The Entrance: Grand or Otherwise

2. The Buddy System

3. The White-Knuckled Drinker—And Other Accessible Folk

4. Name Tags That Pull

5. Great Opening Lines

6. Moving In: Breaking and Entering

7. Moving On: Extricating Yourself

RoAne's Reminders

So, What Do You Say Next?

1. Read One Newspaper a Day

2. Clip and Collect

3. Read Newsletters, Professional Journals and Minutes

4. Take Note and Take Notes

5. Use Humor (Surely You Jest)

6. Listen Actively, Not Passively

7. Just Say Yes to New Opportunities

Five Fundamental Laws of Casual Conversation

Five Fatal Flaws of Casual Conversation

PREFACE

It's been over a dozen years since I first wrote *How to Work a Room,* and the world has changed immensely. Over a million people around the world bought my book because some things just don't change! One of the constant tenets is that we still get invited to events, parties, meetings and conferences—and want to be comfortable, confident, competent and successful.

The need to meet, mingle, make contacts and conversation is even more important in the twenty-first century's Internet working world. Dr. Nathan Keyfitz's prediction came true. As Harvard professor emeritus of sociology in the mid-eighties, he said that "in the year 2000, we will all be technically adept, but who will succeed will be *the people who can talk to other people.*" With social skills on the decline, those that have them will shine in any room.

"Talk"—conversation—is how we relate, explain, persuade, sell, converse, amuse, learn, motivate and **connect.** No matter what walk of life we pursue, we need to be able to break the ice, approach strangers, and start, build and maintain conversations. We cannot build strategic partnerships, business and social relationships and business-to-business models unless we communicate.

- We cannot approach "team building" unless there is an exchange of words among the members of the team.
- We cannot enjoy the benefits of brainstorming unless we are conversing.
- We cannot build a base of customers unless we are communicating.
- We cannot sell our services or products unless we can discuss them.

According to William Strauss, coauthor of *The Fourth Turning: An American Prophecy in the 21st Century,* "Face-to-face contact with bosses, employees, customers will become newly important." That makes mingling, conversing and connecting necessary skills.

This revised and updated edition contains four new chapters to assist you in working actual rooms and virtual ones, as well as a new "Frequently Asked Questions" section, and more quizzes, tips and ideas. A room full of people, especially of strangers, is *still* a daunting experience—even more so today. Why? Because we spend an inordinate amount of time communicating online. We have let our "fingers do the talking" and have lost the skill, courage and confidence to deal with the "face-to-face." We are addicted to E-mail, bulletin boards, chat rooms and E-commerce, thereby decreasing our ability to chat in a room or at an event.

In the 1980s Dr. Phillip Zimbardo of Stanford University's Shyness Clinic discovered that 80 percent of adults identify themselves as shy. In 1995 that figure increased to 88 percent, due in part to technology. We can get money "out of a hole in the wall: the ATM"—that's where kids think money comes from; the "tree" thing is history—and never have to exchange pleasantries with a teller.

We can get our stamps via the Internet, our groceries can be self-checked or ordered from the Web and we can "talk" to people's voicemail without ever having a conversation. These changes impact and decrease day-to-day social conversation skills.

It follows that shyness is currently in the limelight. In 1999 it was the cover story in *U.S. News & World Report, New Republic,* made headlines in *The Wall Street Journal* and was a lead story in *The New York Times.* Why? Because the pharmaceutical companies have discovered the "shy" population as a market for their "meds." Shy or not, we still have to interact in business and social situations to enhance the quality of our lives. To lessen our reticence and reluctance to mix and mingle, *How to Work a Room* is a far better remedy.

When I ask my audiences how many of them feel comfortable in a room full of strangers, it is *rare* that even 5 percent raise their hands—even among salespeople. If they are already sitting in a meeting, attending a convention, at a board retreat, a yearly conference or involved in a keynote presentation, they are already in a group and just need some strategies, tips, opening and exit lines and, mostly, the **permission** to talk to those still unknown colleagues, cronies, contacts, clients, customers and potential friends.

How to Work a Room (Part Deux) provides the impetus, along with many new, improved, tried-and-true strategies, examples and ideas to work any room, gleamed over a dozen years from conversations with hundreds of audiences and feedback from over a million readers.

I am often asked how to converse with someone who is disinterested, bored or aloof. One of the realities of life is that we will not click with everyone we meet. Their timing, interests, agendas and values may be very different from ours. But the rooms will be full of other nice, interesting, friendly people who will be open to meeting, conversing and doing business with us.

If you are in situations where being able to "work" and feel comfortable in any room is important professionally or personally, this book is for you. It contains quizzes, quotes, quips and cartoons. (WARNING: My penchant for puns and wordplay has increased over these dozen years.) If you have a sense of humor, this book's for you. If you suffer from "irony deficiency," especially when you have to attend a conference, party, fundraiser or trade show, this book is the perfect antidote!

ACKNOWLEDGMENTS

Writing a book felt like giving birth to an elephant—and still feels that way. The stretch marks are huge, but I was never alone . . . either time.

Thousands of people gave me their time, energy, insight and humor in personal interviews, conversations and audience feedback. Friends, clients and colleagues as well as people I met on planes, around pools, in line at the supermarket or "treading on the mills" at the health club were generous with their whys, wisdom, wherefores, wit and wonderment.

And thanks to my friends, who support me, believe in me and let me hibernate, exit and reenter as required. I am especially grateful to Terri Skov, Dan Maddux, Pam Martens, Rich Portland, Dr. Geraldine Alpert—and to Aileen Jett RoAne, my late former mother-in-law, who first told me that I should write a book. Thanks also to Pat Teal, Mark Chimsky, Michael LeBoeuf, Dr. Alb, Susan Suffes, Lois Keenan, Patricia Fripp, Toni Boyle, Diane Parente, Connie Ginser and Carol Costello.

To Lana Teplick, chief of staff and best friend, for total support, timely reminders and her "Oh, wow!"s.

To Joyce "Mumsy" Siegel for constant support, laughter and "rye."

To Judith Briles, who first recognized *How to Work a Room* should be a book.

To Sally Osmun for helping me "nail" the necessary!

Especially to Carl LaMell, the chairman of the board of The RoAne Group, for making me find "my baby" a new home.

And to Joann Davis for always believing this book has an audience.

To Jean Miller, who made me attend the American Library Association trade show with my original proposal . . . to find a publisher.

To Jon Tandler, attorney and friend, for guidance and support during my "brown lipstick moments."

To Zach Schisgal, my former editor, for being a good sport with a great sense of humor.

To Edwin Tan, my current editor, for embracing my "baby" and me.

To Becky Gordon, patient transcriber of hieroglyphics.

To Annie Cohen, who "saw" this as a bestseller and made sure it was first published.

To the transgressors of good taste and good behavior, whom I cannot name. I so appreciate the volumes of material they contributed—unwittingly.

Merci beaucoup, muchas gracias, todah rabah, thank you to the unsung heroes of book sales: the sales reps without whom this book would not be in the stores or in your hands; the booksellers who have been so supportive of my "baby" and kind to me these past twelve years.

And to the readers and members of my audiences, who have thanked me these dozen years for helping them manage to mingle more successfully.

INTRODUCTION

You can tell by the feel of the envelope that it's an invitation to *something,* and you're right. One of your clients is the honorary chairperson for a local charity, and they are throwing a huge fund-raiser in two weeks. Not only *should* you go, but many potential clients, opportunities and investors will be there and it's a chance to meet people and promote your business.

Sounds like fun. But before you even have a chance to think about it, a little voice in the back of your head pipes up, "Wait a minute . . . You'll walk into that enormous ballroom and see thousands of strangers! They'll all know one another, but no one will know you. Who will you talk to? What will you say?" Your teeth start to grind and you gingerly place the invitation in your "Wait and See" file or the "circular" one.

You are not alone. This scenario happens daily in offices and homes across the country. It doesn't matter whether the invitation is for a purely social event, a business gathering or a combination of the two—it's uncomfortable for most of us to walk into a room full of people we don't know, especially when we want to make a good impression.

It's also one of the best business and social opportunities we'll ever run across. The benefits of being able to "work" a room with ease and grace are enormous. Here are some of the benefits of being a mingling maven (see Glossary):

- You feel better about yourself. You approach business or social gatherings with enthusiasm and confidence, knowing that this is an arena where you feel comfortable and productive.

- You make invaluable business contacts, as well as starting friendships that may last your whole life. If you hadn't been able to walk up to people, smile, put out your hand and say "Hi!" those opportunities might have been lost.

- You make other people feel more comfortable, which makes them want to know and possibly do business with you and refer business to you.

I have rewritten this book with one goal in mind: to give you the confidence and the tools to walk into any room and **shine**—whether the event is social or professional, a meeting, party, reunion, PTA committee or the Inaugural Ball. This book is designed to help you manage these events successfully, mingle with ease and come away feeling that you have accomplished your own goals—and made other people feel good in the process—and have had a good time.

The focus will be on:

- identifying the "roadblocks" that inhibit us from circulating with ease and comfort, and then eliminating them
- providing a "remedy" to neutralize each roadblock
- strengthening confidence and projecting your warmth, interest and sincerity, which will invite people to open up
- practical tips and strategies for starting conversations, establishing communication and building rapport with "strangers"

In the twenty-first century, those who have the personal touch will profit professionally. Working a room can be your number one marketing strategy. Visibility marketing is some of the best advertising you can get . . . and it's free.

All of us work rooms. If you've ever been to a wedding, a reunion or a meeting, you've worked a room—or else come to have a deep appreciation of how much easier and more pleasant life would be if you developed this skill. People in my audiences and at book signings tell me that the most upsetting thing about these events is that everyone *else* seems to be completely comfortable. Trust me, they only "appear" to be having a grand time.

Most people don't like entering a room full of strangers for any reason. "A party with strangers" is the number one social fear, according to a study on social anxiety reported in *The New York Times*. Most of us would rather speak in public (fear number two) than attend an event with people we don't know.

It might even be said that if you didn't have some anxiety about this, *you would not be normal.*

Most of us want to feel comfortable with other people, even strangers, and will do whatever it takes to minimize the anxiety and move through a crowded room with ease and grace. We want to be comfortable, and make other people feel comfortable with us. We want to "manage the mingling" so that we have fun, feel good about ourselves, score some professional points and feel that even "putting in an appearance" is a good use of our time, especially since time is a commodity that is precious.

"Working a room" is an old political phrase that conjures up images of overweight men in smoky back rooms pressing flesh and cutting deals. But that's not what we mean by it today; today's definition of "working" a room is: *the ability to circulate comfortably and graciously through a gathering of people: meeting, greeting and talking with as many of them as you wish; creating communication that is warm and sincere; establishing an honest rapport on which you can build a professional or personal relationship; and knowing how to start, how to continue and how to end lively and interesting conversations.*

Networking is a different, though interrelated, activity. It is a reciprocal process that is mutually beneficial, where we share leads, ideas and information, and it enhances our personal and professional lives and involves follow-up behaviors that create ongoing connections.

There is nothing inherently calculated or manipulative about "working" a room. However, if you don't really care for and about people, or your warmth, your openness or your desire to connect with them are not genuine, then no technique in the world will help! People sense the truth; they usually know when they are being manipulated, because you have an agenda or want to make a sale. They also know when you are making a sincere effort to extend yourself to them, and they appreciate it.

My guideline is: Go to have fun and enjoy the people there. The professional benefits will follow. But *go!*

Working a room is a risk, no doubt about it. Our egos are on the line, and that can be intimidating. It can also be tremendously rewarding, on both a personal and a professional level.

This book is about understanding what keeps us from approaching these events with ease and enthusiasm, and about what we can do to make them comfortable, pleasant, profitable and even fun. It is about giving ourselves permission to work (not overwork!) every room we enter, and to reap the benefits—both personal and professional. This book will focus on social skills, not cross-cultural communication, in the United States. There are other very fine books that specialize on that topic.

Practice really does make perfect. I encourage you to attend as many events as you can and to practice the techniques in this book. Some will work well, and others may not be right for you. But as Mom always said, "Couldn't hurt to try!" No one ever died from eating spinach . . . or from going to a charity fund-raiser.

You may find that you already know some of the information in this book or that you already practice some of the techniques. Good! Let the book serve as a reminder, and sharpen your skills as you go along. The more you practice, the better you'll be.

And above all—enjoy!

GET
READY!

I

THE FIVE ROADBLOCKS: MOTHER'S DIRE WARNINGS

If working a room is so much fun and so profitable, why do our hearts thump, our palms sweat and our eyes glaze over when we think about it? One reason is that 88 percent of us think of ourselves as shy. When we get invited to a meeting, conference or party, we shy away from the opportunity in order to avoid the discomfort.

Another reason is that many years ago we were taught *not* to talk to strangers. Mom gave us these dire warnings with the best of intentions, "for our own good," and everybody agreed that we should heed them. The trouble is, they worked a lot better when we were six years old than they do now that we are twenty-six, forty-six or sixty-six.

Now that we're no longer walking home alone from first grade, these dire warnings have changed from safety barriers into roadblocks that prevent us from mingling comfortably and effectively with other people. Mom isn't to blame. But we heard these warnings so often—and perhaps repeated them to our own kids so often—that they became a way of life.

There are five major roadblocks to working a room successfully. Knowing where they come from is the first step to letting go of them.

ROADBLOCK #1
"DON'T TALK TO STRANGERS"

This first roadblock is as American as apple pie. It is often accompanied by a shaking of the index finger. It made sense when our mothers did this to us, and it makes sense when we do it to our children. We *still* don't want our children to talk to strangers on the way home from school today more than ever.

But it *doesn't* make sense when we're selling a product at a trade show, beginning our first day on a new job, attending a formal ball or mingling at a professional-association meeting or convention where contacts and connections are standing six deep around the room. Yet we often find ourselves standing in the door, paralyzed, with that imaginary finger shaking in our faces and the message "Don't talk to strangers" flashing across our subconscious. So, we don't.

Instead, we choose a nice, quiet spot at the hors d'oeuvres table and start nibbling, get very busy with a cup of coffee or a drink, smile nervously around the room at no one in particular—and have an awful time. Or we hang out on the periphery of the room . . . against the walls. (Hence the term "wallflower.")

The problem is that we also miss tremendous business, career and social opportunities. Who knows what wonderful person or valuable contact was standing in that room feeling just as uncomfortable as we were?

Life is too short, and time too precious, to spend an hour or two squandering opportunities and, in the process, having a bad time.

ROADBLOCK #2
"WAIT TO BE PROPERLY INTRODUCED" (THE SCARLETT O'HARA SYNDROME)

Imagine Scarlett, standing on the steps of Tara in all its antebellum glory, batting her eyelashes as she drawls, "My, but we haven't been properly introduced." Her beauty and charm notwithstanding, Scarlett wouldn't have gotten very far at a professional association meeting. In Scarlett's day and social sphere, everyone was very much aware of proper introductions and there were people, usually older women, who did little else. They would make *sure* you met that gallant, dark-haired man or that stunning belle or the local banker who might be interested in your crop expansion.

But tomorrow did, indeed, become "another day" and now you can't count on personal or professional "matchmakers" to be sure you are introduced around at the political meeting or the reception after the lecture.

Yet many of us were taught that it "wasn't nice" to talk to someone unless we had been introduced by a mutual acquaintance. It is certainly *easier* to begin a conversation when you've been formally introduced. At the very least, you have in common the person who introduced you. "How do you know Leslie?" elicits more information about the person you've just met, and can lead to other subjects of conversation.

But at most events we can't count on being introduced to anyone, let alone the people we most want to meet. We may be on our own when it comes to circulating, and we may have to walk up to people and introduce *ourselves*. If we don't want to be left standing in the middle of the room, staring at the ceiling or the floor, we have to realize that Scarlett had her world and we have ours . . . and send her packing back to Tara.

ROADBLOCK #3
"DON'T BE PUSHY. GOOD THINGS COME TO THOSE WHO WAIT." (THE PROM KING/QUEEN COMPLEX)

Let's face it. The world may beat a path to the door of Prom Kings and Queens, but not everyone is royal. And once the Prom is over, even the ex-Kings and ex-Queens can't always afford to sit back and hope that people will seek them out.

As we watched the Kings and Queens being besieged with dates, Mom told us, "Good things come to those who wait." *Au contraire* . . . gray hair comes to those who wait, and sometimes even varicose veins if the waiting is done standing up!

Waiting for people to find you and introduce themselves is an exercise in futility. Chances are, they won't—because it's just as difficult for them as it is for you. Because 88 percent of us are shy and won't initiate, the "waiting game" is a colossal waste of time, no fun at all and murder on your self-esteem.

It reminds me of myself and legions of other current

and former teenagers who sat by the phone and stared at it, waiting for it to ring. I learned the hard way that it did *not* work for the Prom. Why would I expect it to work now? If it were not for my mom, Lil, and Larry Katzen's mom, Marion, I'd still be waiting for my prom date to call!

Even the inventor who actually does build a better mousetrap has to get out there and let people know about it. If he doesn't, he'll sit at home for the rest of his life with no mice, but no fame nor fortune either. He might as well have bought a cat.

People who "wait for others to come to them" can often be found in the corner of the room, holding up the walls, envying those who glide around the reception or the cocktail party meeting people.

And let's talk about "pushy." There is pushy, and there is pushy. Obviously, you don't want to throw yourself into a stranger's arms or pin him down on the conference table, wagging your finger in his face and forcing fistfuls of business cards into his pockets. That's one thing. It's quite another to approach someone in a pleasant, friendly way, to smile, introduce yourself and say something like, "This is my first meeting. Is there always such a good turnout?"

People who fall victim to the Prom King/Queen Complex and sit around waiting for the world to find them are often perceived as aloof, even arrogant, when they may be feeling uncomfortable or shy. They may or may not actually *be* shy, but that is how they've come to think of themselves.

In one of my early jobs as an elementary school teacher, I found that these labels often became self-fulfilling prophecies. The "Troublemaker" of the class always found a way to maintain that dubious distinction. The "Talker" (today's conversationalist) always managed to get the most red checks next to "Keeps Profitably Busy." (I'm afraid I fell into this category, but to this day I can't imagine anything more compelling about school than social intercourse with my classmates. Multiplication tables? Diagramming sentences? Give me note-passing and furtive whispering in the back row!)

Shyness can be a learned response, according to Dr. Lynne Kelly, a University of Hartford professor who specializes in the study of shyness ("Professor Treats Problem of Shyness," *The New York Times,* February 3, 1985). The young child who hides when Auntie Glynda wants to hug him hello hears Mom or Dad say, "He's just shy." Aha! Now he figures out how to get out of these interactions with Auntie, and the label sticks! What we learn, we can unlearn. Working on both communication and conversation skills is one way of unlearning shyness.

"Most people experience 'situational shyness,'" says Dr. Philip Zimbardo, author of *Shyness and What to Do About It.* Certain situations make all of us feel reticent. We may be as shy about an important sales meeting, a product review or a child's parent-teacher conference as we feel about walking into the grand ballroom of a major hotel and having a thousand people turn their heads in our direction.

But with training, practice and the refining of our communication skills, shyness can be reduced or eliminated altogether.

Leaders and other successful people have learned to overcome their shyness. They don't wait; they reach out and extend themselves to people. In *The Magic of Thinking Big,* Dr. David Schwartz says, "It's a mark of real leadership to take the lead in getting to know people. . . . It's always a big person who walks up to you and offers his/her hand and says hello."

ROADBLOCK #4
"BETTER SAFE THAN SORRY"
(RISKING REJECTION)

So you work up your nerve and approach a stranger. You smile, say hello and introduce yourself. The other person casts you a disinterested glance that screams "WHO CARES?"

This hurts. No one wants to be rebuffed or ignored to their face. Our egos are on the line when we extend ourselves to others, because there is always the possibility that they won't be interested in talking with us.

But Mother's dire warning that we're "better safe than sorry" puts a real damper on risk, and **risk is the name of the game when you are working a room.**

I like to think of this risk as a challenge. If you don't have anything on the table, you never win. If you don't take the risk and reach out to people, you never make new friends or new contacts. Most of us are strong enough to withstand a temporarily chipped ego. We risk our lives all the time on the freeway and some of the same people who participate in risky Xtreme sports (mountain climbing, bunjee jumping, sky diving, etc.) are those for whom a roomful of people is too much of a risk.

The truth is, very few people will be openly hostile or rude—if for no reason other than that it's bad business. The person who appears to be disinterested may not be judging or rejecting us . . . but thinking of another worry. Mother may have fallen and broken a hip and the family has to make a convalescent-care decision or the company may be merging and downsizing possibilities loom. Or that person who seems so distant may be one who is much shyer and less confident than you.

ROADBLOCK #5
"MANGLED AND MIXED MESSAGES"

We run the risk that our warm, open, friendly manner will be misconstrued as an invitation to a liaison. Women are especially vulnerable to this misinterpretation. A touch on the arm that is intended as a simple gesture of understanding can be misconstrued as an indication of sexual interest or intrusion.

Although Mother's warning is a bit extreme, we have to go about our lives, be very clear with ourselves about our intent and exercise a bit of caution in this area. In the past twelve years, sexual harassment has become a topic and behavior of concern. It makes sense to be aware of the issues, and still be open and friendly. We need to keep our hands to ourselves and watch our language, including our "Honey Dos and Don'ts."

RISKING THE ROADBLOCKS

These five roadblocks are part of what stop us from min-gling, circulating and working a room. In the next chap-ter, we'll discuss specific remedies for each roadblock.

But there is something else that can stop us from moving comfortably around a room, something subtler than the five particular roadblocks we've just discussed. It has to do with self-perception, self-confidence and self-esteem. People who register low in these areas can talk themselves out of meeting people and feeling at ease talk-ing to them.

In *Talking to Yourself,* Dr. Pamela Butler dealt with the concept of self-talk, which has become more widely rec-ognized in the last twelve years. These are the things we say to ourselves in our minds, sometimes without even being aware that we are saying them. Self-talk can be either positive or negative. Dr. Butler says that we can change negative self-talk to positive self-talk, and that this transformation can have benefits in all areas of our lives.

It works! I attended a party and met a nice couple. The wife told me that before her marriage her profes-sional networking group used my book for their discus-sion forum. She committed to revising her "self-talk" and attended a party. She saw a nice man whom she learned was single and struck up a conversation about their host, which led to other topics of interest. That nice man? You guessed it . . . her husband! Yenta the Matchmaker takes her bow.

Here is some negative self-talk that might come up when you think of working a room:

- I've always had trouble meeting people. It's just the way I am.

- I can't make—and don't like—small talk.

- I don't have anything important or interesting to say. I'll just embarrass myself. Better to keep quiet and be cool.

- Why would anyone want to listen to me? All these people have more important things to do.

Take a moment to write down any negative self-talk you may have, and then rewrite those statements as positive ones. The above comments might be rewritten as:

- I'm having fun practicing meeting people, and getting better at it all the time. I'm enjoying mastering a new skill.

- Small talk is a great way to get to know new people.

- I want to extend myself to other people and know that the most valuable thing I have to offer is myself. If I'm open and honest, I'll feel good about myself and so will they.

- We're all busy, but everyone enjoys connecting with other people. I'm a valuable, likable person. Extending myself is a gift that others appreciate.

AN ELEVATING EXPERIENCE

One of the "rooms" that really confounds us is the elevator. Should we talk to the boss? the chairman of the board? or the stranger? Have a pleasantry prepared and a smile for the times it appears to be appropriate. However, there are times when your courageous conversation may interrupt the boss lost in thought. Doing something outrageous, an antic or a "shtick" (see Glossary), may backfire. What we want to be is outgoing . . . being too outrageous could make us appear foolish and that does not enhance our careers. Assess each situation on a case-by-case basis.

CHANGE/RISK/REWARD

Change of any kind is a risk and feels uncomfortable—even when the change is for the good. It's a little sad to leave the old house, even when we're moving into a much nicer one. We leave behind the old, familiar ways and step onto new ground. No matter how wonderful the change—getting married, expanding your business, moving to an exciting new city, switching careers—there is always a certain amount of discomfort.

For most of us, working a room is a change. **But extending ourselves to people is almost always worth the risk.** When we try and succeed, it makes us feel like a million dollars. But when we allow negative self-talk to prevail, we can become overwhelmed by the roadblocks talk ourselves out of taking a risk.

If we don't seize the moment, it will be gone . . . along with the opportunity.

How many times have you seen someone who looked vaguely familiar but were afraid to go over because he might not be who you thought he was? I say, so what if I *am* wrong? The worst that can happen is that he says he's not that person and I've made a new acquaintance— possibly a new friend.

In 1981 I attended my first meeting of a local professional association. One of the men there looked like a person I had met the previous June at a career training conference. He was standing alone at the bar. Several questions raced through my mind when I saw him. What if he wasn't the man I had met, but just a look-alike? Would he think I was coming on to him? On the other hand, what if he really *was* the person I'd met and felt slighted because I didn't recognize him? Should I go up and say hello, or wait for him to come to me?

Of all these possibilities, I decided that the worst result would be that he was the person I'd met and thought I was ignoring him. My value system, which includes more than a mild dose of guilt, took over. I approached Farrell Chiles and mentioned the June conference. He was *not* the person I had met, but we had a pleasant conversation.

OLD LINES: NEW FRIENDS

He had been following the original "Careers" series in the *San Francisco Examiner* and remembered several of my columns. That made me feel terrific. I was very glad that I'd overcome my reluctance to approach him. The benefits have been immeasurable. We play significant roles in each other's networks and we have been friends since then. Since that encounter, we tell the story of our unique first meeting, and always pay tribute to that great old line, "Don't I know you from someplace?"

CORRALLING YOUR COURAGE

No one can give you the courage to introduce yourself to a stranger. But some people are more supportive of this behavior than others. My advice: Stick with those who encourage you to take the initiative.

One way to muster up the courage to take a risk is to ask yourself, "What's the worst that can happen?" Surprisingly enough, your worst fear is usually *not* a matter of life and death. And the odds are that disaster will not occur—and that even if it does, you will survive.

Taking the risk is almost always worth the discomfort. It's a cliché, but "nothing ventured, nothing gained." With technology moving the world at warp speed, embracing real-time opportunities for face-to-face connections makes sense.

ROANE'S REMINDERS

"Mother's Dire Warnings" still lurk in our subconscious. These five roadblocks can prevent us from making the most of a party or a business event. When we know what they are, we can remedy them.

1. Don't talk to strangers.
2. Wait to be properly introduced. (The Scarlett O'Hara Syndrome)
3. Don't be pushy. Good things come to those who wait. (The Prom King/Queen Complex)
4. Better safe than sorry. (Risking Rejection)
5. Mangled and Mixed Messages (The Intercepted Pass)

Advisories:
- Be aware of negative self-talk and change it into positive self-talk.
- Extending yourself to people feels risky, but the benefits are well worth the discomfort.

2

THE REMEDIES: REMOVING THE ROADBLOCKS

Now for the good news: For every roadblock, there is a remedy. Those dire warnings can stop us at any time, unless we apply the appropriate remedy.

REMEDY #1
REDEFINE THE TERM "STRANGER"

Mom says not to talk to strangers? Okay, let's redefine the term. Obviously, we have to exercise some caution in today's society. Not every street corner in town is a suitable place to mix and mingle. And there will always be some people who, for some inexplicable reason, make you feel very uneasy. Go with your gut reaction; it's a great guide.

But if you are attending a meeting of professional colleagues, you're not really with strangers. If you go to a PTA meeting, you may not know anyone in the room, but you all have a common interest in quality education for your children. When you go to a new health club, a new church, a new synagogue, a new charitable or political organization, a computer trade show, you have a *common interest* with those people.

When you go to a party, you probably know the host or hostess. At a wedding, you have some connection with the bride or groom. At a baseball game, notice how everyone talks to everyone else who is rooting for the same team.

Think about what you have in common with people at an event **before** you get there. This is the planning that helps you feel more comfortable and more prepared. You share interests, issues or government regulations with anyone who does the same kind of work you do, who is interested in your work or whose work interests you. People who sell respirators, perform surgery, repair medical equipment and process insurance have a common bond. They all deal with hospitals. If you volunteer for the local United Way, March of Dimes or public radio station, you have an interest in common with both the other volunteers and the people who volunteer for other organizations.

People who have children have a common bond— whether they are construction engineers, musicians, used-car salesmen or company presidents.

> *These common interests can be the basis for conversation.* Understanding what we have in common with others takes the edge off our reluctance to approach them as "strangers."

A friend of mine attended a formal fund-raiser for his son's school and, in talking with another father whom he knew from Little League, discovered that the other dad's work was executive search. A happy coincidence, since my friend was planning a career change!

Use common sense when approaching people you don't know, but loosen up the definition of "stranger" so that Mother's Dire Warnings don't keep you from establishing contacts and communication. Whether you're at a charity awards banquet, a spouse's company dinner dance or your child's soccer team play-offs, **identifying the common ground can help you break the ice.**

You will feel more comfortable, and that will be your reward for changing a behavior and breaking through a roadblock.

REMEDY #2
PRACTICE A SELF-INTRODUCTION

Scarlett O'Hara may have needed a "proper introduction," but we live in a different world. We may never meet another living soul if we wait for a Fairy Godperson magically to appear and introduce us around. We'll just stand in the corner, watching the real "room workers" who seem totally comfortable moving around the room, meeting strangers, conversing and circulating through the crowd.

Every so often, you actually get lucky and attend an event that has a greeting committee. The problem is, not everyone on the committee knows who you are, who you want to meet or how to introduce people properly—so they may not be able to give you much of an introduction, and they may not introduce you to the people you want to meet. Don't let yourself be limited by their lack of skills, their lack of information, their lack of contacts or all three.

The truth is that we are on our own. Therefore, we need to have a *planned* and *practiced* self-introduction that is clear, interesting and well-delivered.

What you say about yourself will depend on the nature of the event. At a chamber of commerce reception, for example, you could say your name and what you do—with energy. But at a purely social function, your occupation may not be as important as how you know the host or hostess. **Your self-introduction should be tailored to the event.**

When I attended a wedding in Chicago, for instance, I didn't use my business introduction as a best-selling author and professional speaker—although I was prepared with business cards in my evening bag. Instead, I said warmly (and carefully, because it was a bit of a tongue twister), "I'm the first girlfriend of the father of the groom!" Trust me, conversations started!

A good self-introduction includes your name and something about yourself that establishes what you have in common with the other people at the event. It doesn't have to be long, only about seven to nine seconds. But your self-introduction should give the essential information, and perhaps something interesting that may engage people in conversation. Patricia Fripp, professional speaker and speech coach, recommends that you give the benefit of what you do rather than your job title. "This allows the others to ask a question or make a comment that moves the conversation forward. And you have engaged them."

- "Hello. I'm Jack Jones. I help people 'take stock' of their lives." (Stockbroker)
- "Hello. I'm Judy Farley, former roommate of the bride."
- "Hello. I'm Shelly Berger. This is my first meeting, and I'm feeling a bit awkward."

Once you have planned how to introduce yourself, practice. You'll feel much more at ease with it and have a wonderfully effective remedy for the Scarlett O'Hara Syndrome.

REMEDY #3
MOVE FROM "GUEST" BEHAVIOR TO "HOST" BEHAVIOR

Remember the Prom King/Queen Complex, and Mother's Dire Warning not to be pushy? There is no need to get gray hair waiting for "good things to come to you."

> *RoAne's Cliché Cure:*
> *Good things don't come to those who wait.*
> *Good things come to those who initiate!*

Dr. Adele Scheele, author of *Skills for Success,* says that people in a social or networking situation tend to behave either as "hosts" or as "guests."

Whether it's talking to a stranger at an event, making an introductory phone call or posting your resumé on a job search website, actions create more actions and often positive interactions.

The "hosts" exhibit gracious manners—meeting people, starting conversations, introducing others and making sure that their needs are met. "Hosts" are concerned with the comfort of others and actively contribute to that comfort.

"Guest" behavior is just the opposite. "Guests" wait for someone to take their coats, offer them a drink and introduce them around the room. Often, the wait is interminable. If no one performs these services for them, "guests" move to the corners of the room and stand there until someone rescues them. They may be suffering the agonies of shyness, but other people interpret their behavior as "standoffish."

Dr. Scheele suggests that the key to success is moving from "guest" behavior to "host" behavior; this has been identified as the most valuable "tip" from my audiences and readers, whether they were CEOs, engineers or hedge-fund managers.

We all have it in us to be "hosts." Some people have developed their "hosting" skills more than others, but all of us have some level of what I call "innate host behavior" that we can build upon.

GUESTS AND A "HOST" OF BEHAVIORS

What exactly do hosts do? Basically, the host's job is to extend himself or herself to the guests and make them feel comfortable. If you are having company or throwing a party, you plan a guest list and a menu. You clean out the hall closet. When the guests arrive, you welcome them at the door, take their coats and invite them in. You smile and greet them. You offer them food and get them something to drink. You introduce them around, mentioning the things they have in common with other people. You provide conversation starters, perhaps an interesting story or piece of information about the guest. At the end of the evening, you retrieve their coats and thank each guest for coming.

In myriad presentations, attendees have said the most memorable trait of a host is the person who introduces us to others . . . matchmakers, of a sort.

These are things that most of us have done, but we may be out of practice. It may be time to dust off those social skills and start practicing them at public events.

The only way to move from "guest" to "host" behavior at events is to DO IT. Try one behavior at a time. I may sound like a Pollyanna, but when we focus on someone else's comfort before our own, it takes the onus off us and we are more comfortable.

Volunteering to be on the greeting committee of your organization is one way to meet everyone who comes in the door; it's your *job* to meet people and make them feel comfortable. You have something specific to do, and it is just the thing you want to do anyway—meet and connect with people. You have an excuse to be as outgoing as you want to be. And the benefits are bountiful. At a meeting of the Northern California National Speakers Association, I saw a woman who looked very nice and yet uncomfortable standing alone. I remembered how daunting my first meeting was, so I introduced myself and welcomed her. Lee Robert and I have been dear friends ever since. Our conversations over time have laid a foundation of a firm, heartfelt connection that has strengthened our loving friendship.

CAUTION:: "Acting" as a host will not be successful if it is, indeed, an act. If you really don't care about the people you meet and greet, it will be very evident. "Acting warmly" is self-contradictory. Either you is . . . or you isn't.

Moving from "guest" to "host" behavior is the perfect remedy for the Prom King/Queen Complex. It makes the meeting or the evening *your* event. You feel more comfortable extending yourself to others because it is your *job* and others are naturally drawn to you.

REMEDY #4
EJECT THE "REJECTOR" AND MOVE ON

Fear of rejection is sometimes a self-fulfilling prophecy. When we're afraid people will reject us, we sometimes avoid them so that it doesn't happen. Even when it comes at us from out of the blue, it's hard to take. It's no fun to put yourself out, extend a hand and a smile, introduce yourself and get a withering stare in return. Remember, give people a second chance because their thoughts may be elsewhere.

The only advice I can offer in response to this kind of rude behavior is to *move on*. If there is no chemistry or interest, we should not waste our time trying to convince anyone to converse with us. There are other nice people in the room who would be open to meeting us.

Instead, simply excuse yourself and walk away. The other person's behavior probably has nothing to do with you. The shy person may not know what to say. The pre-occupied person is just that.

Respond to this kind of behavior as you would a deadly flu bug—and fly the coop!

REMEDY #5
UNMIX THE MIXED MESSAGE

With so many men and women working together today, we have to watch our behaviors so that those not intended as sexual will not be misinterpreted as such. However, there are several things you can do to prevent your words, gestures, clothing and manner from being perceived as improper.

The first is to ask yourself if your behavior really *is* being misinterpreted or whether you actually do have an interest in this person. If your interest really is romantic, face the truth yourself and proceed in a way that won't jeopardize your professional relationship.

Unmixing the Signals We Send

- Don't dress for misperception. Avoid see-through blouses and Ally McBeal–like short skirts and other suggestive clothing in the office.

- Stay away from double entendres and off-color comments.

- Be conscious of body language.

- Be clear about your purpose. Stick to business.

- You might even want to "lose your touch" a bit, at least in situations where it is apt to be misinterpreted.

We can't control others' thoughts and actions, but we can be aware of the signals we send—and of whether or not we want to send them. Let's not contribute to the confusion.

Continue to be friendly and outgoing . . . just be aware.

The differences between male and female behavior patterns, motivations and conversation are well documented in research. Dr. Deborah Tannen's body of work reflects these issues. In the last twelve years, the popular literature has addressed these gender differences ad nauseum. *How to Work a Room* is about communicating with many people of myriad differences while building rapport, trust and friendships. Each of these remedies represents a change in behavior, but you will reap the benefits a hundredfold. We'll talk about some of those benefits in the next chapter.

ROANE'S REMINDERS

The good news about the five roadblocks to working a room is that there is a remedy for each one. With a little practice, a little risk-taking and some old-fashioned social graces, those "Dire Warnings" will never again stop you from moving through a room with ease and grace. The added benefits are making good contacts and, most important, having a *great* time!

ROADBLOCK	REMEDY
Don't talk to strangers.	Redefine the term "stranger."
Wait to be properly introduced. (The Scarlett O'Hara Syndrome)	Practice a seven- to nine-second self-introduction.
Don't be pushy. Good things come to those who wait. (The Prom King/ Queen Complex)	Move from "guest" behavior to "host" behavior.
Better safe than sorry. (Risking Rejection)	Eject the rejector and move on.
Mangled and mixed messages. (The Intercepted Pass)	Unmix the mixed messages. Watch words, dress and body language.

BENEFITS: THE BONUSES OF BEING THERE

Have you ever been invited to a dinner, reception or meeting that you couldn't avoid, but that didn't sound very exciting? You write down the event in your calendar, drag yourself there, put in your time and come home feeling as if you've wasted three hours.

With a little planning, that need never happen again. The event doesn't exist that can't be made productive, or at least fun, if we give it a little thought before we go. It doesn't take much time or effort to turn those "chore" events into "choices" when we approach them as adventures into the unknown.

TURNING CHORES INTO CHOICES

To work a room effectively, we need to know why we are doing it. If there is nothing in it for us or for other people, if there is no goal, reason or purpose—why bother? The reason may be as simple as your boss invited you or your client is sponsoring a fund-raiser for the local Leukemia Society or March of Dimes or your nephew is graduating.

If you have decided to attend, you should know WHY. The benefits will vary from room to room, depending on the nature of the event, but you should have a clear purpose for attending. Why have you chosen to spend your time there, instead of surfing the net to do research, watching *South Park,* practicing your golf swing, helping the kids with their homework, going for a run or visiting your relatives?

Only one person can answer these questions: YOU.

PLANNING PAYOFFS

Before you attend an event, ask yourself what you would like to accomplish—both on a professional level and on a personal level.

It's important to identify these benefits *before* the event. Remember that "business" events can have personal benefits as well, and that purely "social" events can do wonders for your business. Think about what you want as rewards or compensation. I use the term "compensation" because deriving a benefit is a payment—or payoff—for expending the energy and investing the time. And "work" is defined as the exertion of energy!

In my speeches and consulting, I give people time to jot down what they feel are the most important personal and professional benefits of working a room. These are the points they make most often:

Professional Payoffs

1. Perceived as powerful and in control
2. Established communication/connections/rapport
3. Increased resource base/potential clients
4. Gained insight; learned new information
5. Increased business opportunities
6. Enhanced career options
7. Had fun!

Yes, fun is a professional benefit. *In fact, the best business minglers often have the most fun,* because they have learned the joys of working a room, and are a joy to talk to in any room. What's not to like about getting new business, feeling good yourself and enjoying other people?

Personal Payoffs

1. Comfort
2. Self-confidence
3. New contacts/friends
4. Newly-acquired knowledge
5. Fun!

THE FUN FACTOR

It's no accident that "FUN" is on both lists. Who would want to spend time commuting, parking, circulating and chatting—just to have a lousy time?

Identifying the potential benefits of a meeting, party, convention or any other event is one of the best ways to motivate, tantalize or prod ourselves into making the most of each event. It builds purpose and confidence, and that leads to even more confidence.

And we're not just there to "get ours." It works both ways. In fact, those who attend events to push forward their agendas are transparent and repellent. Each of us has something to offer other people, and we should focus on our potential contributions as well. We can benefit the other attendees by offering information, advice, an ear, leads, ideas and whatever else seems appropriate or useful to them.

BELIEVING IN THE BENEFITS

It's important to believe in the benefits, to make them real and vital so that they give us energy and spur us on. As with everything else about working a room, identifying the benefits gets easier with practice. I often ask people to think about the last event that they attended. I then ask them to identify, with twenty/twenty hindsight, the benefits to them if they had worked the room effectively. I even give them this short form to fill out. Think of an event you attended recently, and try it yourself.

Benefits

Event _____

Sponsor _____

Purpose _____

Location _____

Attendees _____

Reason for Your Participation _____

_____

Potential Professional Benefits:

1.

2.

3.

4.

5.

Potential Personal Benefits:

1.

2.

3.

4.

5.

The personal benefits can be at least as important as the professional. Even if you never discuss business, the people you meet while working a room can become lasting friends who enrich your life.

The San Francisco Business Times cosponsored a women entrepreneur's award evening. While I met several business contacts, by hanging out at the dessert table the evening was a success for another reason. Three times that night I bumped into the same woman. The third time we laughed and Allison Fortini Baumgarten, an account executive for an online start-up company, said, "Geez, three time's a charm. It must be that we are supposed to meet!" She and I have been friends ever since! Will we do business with each other? As my grandmother always said, "You never know!"

Networking applies to friendships as well as careers. I met a colleague at a National Speakers Association convention, and we stayed in touch. When one of his friends, executive coach Charles Amico, moved to San Francisco, he called me. We have been friends ever since, through good times and some tough ones.

You may have similar stories of chance meetings and networks of friends. If you stop to think about it, many of them probably came from working a room.

ACCUMULATING CONTACTS: THE MILLIONAIRE'S ROLODEX

Being able to work a room effectively has one benefit that is extraordinary and unique: You can build an enormous Rolodex. You're on your way to having something in common with millionaires.

Before he wrote *The Millionaire Next Door,* Thomas Stanley studied two thousand millionaires. He found that the most important trait they had in common was a huge Rolodex! Today it can be online, scanned into your contact management program, downloaded onto your palm . . . or Palm Pilot. But the fact remains, the list of names we have in our Rolodex or database are those with whom we have had *personal* contact! No more *cold* calls or blind, mass e-mails.

He also says that these people have an "uncanny ability to distinguish quality contacts." They don't just collect business cards; they can identify the people who are able and *willing* to help them, the people with whom they can share support, information and, possibly, business. A huge Rolodex is useless unless, like the millionaires Stanley studied, we see it as a resource pool of people, ideas and advice.

Working a room is one sure way to expand your contacts. According to Stanley, these millionaires showed the same guts and courage in talking to people at events as they did in conducting their businesses.

IT WORKS BOTH WAYS

Remember: We sometimes forget that each of us has something to offer. We can benefit the other attendees by offering information, advice, an ear, leads, ideas, etc.

I may not be able to answer a technical or a tax problem, but I can offer ideas on the world of publishing and promotion. And although nobody ever asks me for a recipe, I can suggest a great restaurant. If we make a list of what we know, do, like and have some experience in, we will feel more confident in our ability to contribute.

ROANE'S REMINDERS

- Learn to approach any event with purpose and enthusiasm.

- Identify the potential benefits *before you go.* These benefits can be personal or professional or both.

- Having fun and meeting new friends can be just as valuable as striking deals. (Striking deals can lead to new friends and be a lot of fun!)

- Being a resource to others, not just focused on your agenda, is preferable.

- We all have something to contribute. If we list our preferences, interests and experience, we know what we can offer others!

- As far as results, in the long run . . . "You never know!"

4

THE DYNAMIC DUO: CHARM AND CHUTZPAH

Working a room successfully depends on seeing the road-blocks, responding with the appropriate remedies and identifying the potential benefits. But in the end, what gets us through the night is the dynamic duo of CHARM and CHUTZPAH (see Glossary).

I can hear it now: "Charm and Chutzpah in the same breath? They're a contradiction in terms . . . and behaviors." Not true!

CHUTZPAH—THE COURAGE TO CONVERSE

The old, negative connotations of "chutzpah" are gall, nerve, a brassiness that is intrusive and offensive. To me, chutzpah is not aggression, rudeness, disrespect or bulldozing. It is simply the *courage to take risks.*

Chutzpah allows us to make that first, icebreaking comment, to open the doors to conversation. It gives us the courage to walk into the party, fund-raiser, aerobics class or meeting, take a deep breath and introduce ourselves to someone.

Can it help you work a room? What else *is* working a room?

Would you wish it on your children? You bet! They will be ahead of the game when *they* start working rooms (and they *will*). The socially skilled person will succeed in the twenty-first century and stand out from the crowd.

CHUTZPAH IS THE CORNERSTONE OF CONFIDENCE

In the 1980s, chutzpah had been elevated to the status of a management tool. In "Getting Chutzpah" (*Savvy*, November 1982), psychologist Elliot Jaffa identified chutzpah as an "overlooked personal quality that makes a successful manager."

Jaffee said that chutzpah allows us to risk rejection, ask for what we want and express ourselves. It gives us the strength to pick ourselves up, dust ourselves off and start all over again. It has become "Yinglish," part of our vernacular. It is important to have a dose of chutzpah to get through the day.

Here is what *Webster's* has to say about charm:

Verb: to captivate, delight, attract, please
Noun: a power to gain affection

These definitions make most people shout, "Where do I sign up?"

In "charm" school I was taught how to dress, walk,

apply makeup, smile, behave and be well-mannered. These things are important, but charm includes something more, an elusive quality that draws us to people and makes us believe they care about us. When we charm people, they become comfortable and at ease.

THE CHARMERS

- Katie Couric
- Tom Hanks
- Michael Jordan
- Sophia Loren
- Sammy Sosa

Who Do You Find Charming? Why?

1. _____

2. _____

3. _____

4. _____

5. _____

What do they do that makes you think so?

Once we identify the charming behavior, we can emulate it.

Charm is a combination of warmth, good nature, positive attitude, a good sense of humor, charisma, spirit, energy and an interest in others. My friend and associate Diane Parente has it. She is a consultant and speaker who helps clients define their image. She has a wonderful sense of humor and laughter. People *want* to be around her. Charm is the ability to convey a type of caring that comes from the heart and soul . . . and she does.

An advice columnist once defined "class" as the "ability to make people of all walks of life feel comfortable." To me, that definition also applies to charm.

The Mill Valley Film Festival honored actor Sir Derek Jacobi (*I, Claudius*). At the reception in his honor, Sir Derek greeted each of us with great warmth and made us feel as if he had waited all day to meet us. We, too, should treat people as if we "waited all day to meet them."

When we work a room, a party, a convention or a jogging track, we must be keenly aware of other people's feelings. Ignoring someone because the title on their name tag doesn't impress us is a cardinal sin. During a question and answer session, after one of my presentations, an executive asked how—if that she could only "invest time with decision-makers, could she easily identify them?" This is a question salespeople often ask after being trained by some sales trainers of the old school. I looked at this busy executive, paused and said, "I think there is a commandment against thinking like that. If not, there should be!" So, I wrote it in *The Secrets of Savvy Networking*. How uncharming of her! And foolish. It ignores those who influence "decision-makers" . . . and the fact that they could be the decision-maker next year.

ONE AND ONE IS THREE

When chutzpah and charm come together, it's synergistic. The whole is greater than the sum of its parts. You don't just have chutzpah *and* charm, you have MAGIC!

You care about people, and you have the courage to walk up to them and let them know it. That's a powerful combination, and one that enriches everyone concerned. But, there has to be a balance between the two.

The dynamic duo of chutzpah and charm isn't a "to do" or a technique. It is something we all have, and that we've developed to a greater or lesser extent. Now is the time to let it out and spread it around.

There is no more effective way to work a room or . . . be NICE in a room. People remember the people who make them feel special, comfortable and conversant and whose demeanors make them smile. You'll never have to bring, do or wear attention-getting gimmicks again! Nice is good . . . and memorable.

Some of the new rooms we will work will be virtual ones. Being a savvy online mixer and mingler is important. In the next chapter, the virtual room will be explored.

ROANE'S REMINDERS

- Chutzpah and charm are the dynamic duo at the heart of working a room successfully. We all have these qualities.

- Practice makes them stronger. They let us work a room with style and grace—and, ultimately, are what attract people to us.

- Identify who is charming and why. What do they do and say? Don't do and don't say?

- Emulate them.

5

HOW TO
WORK THE
"VIRTUAL" ROOM

The chitchat about chat rooms has exploded since I first wrote about it in 1995. We now have several generations of people whose virtual socializing, conversing and networking has exceeded their real time they spend on each activity. With that, we have lost a lot of our personal touch.

The online world not only gives us a new type of room to work, we also get thousands of possible "rooms" in which to chat about anything, anywhere, anytime. It's a room without the boundaries of walls or time, yet there are rules and boundaries of better behavior to be observed.

There are myriad stories of people finding long-lost relatives, friends, even romance (one of my friends married a chat room friend!); of seniors whose frailties keep them homebound, of those who stay in touch with a grandchild or find a community online, of those suffering from similar symptoms, or those who find an online support group or are just pals. For the record, the largest-growing segment of the online world is senior citizens. Chat rooms can and do create a community—a virtual one.

There are also stories of the dangers of meeting "online friends." Exercising caution is important.

A chat room is a subject or an interest-based "room" and can vary in size (numbers of visitors) from moment to moment. When someone enters, their entry is heralded by a notice/greeting. Sometimes individuals will greet you, other times not. It is best to observe the conversation before jumping into a monologue on your favorite subject.

THE MYSTIQUE

Anonymity is a feature of the online world, where only e-mail handles are used. Hiding behind a name, a pseudonym, if you will, runs counter to the concept of heartfelt conversation. It's difficult enough that we hear no tone, no inflections, see no facial expressions, but we now have no idea with whom we are really chatting. But once we discover other Trekkies, classical-jazz fans, fellow meeting planners, mountain bikers, grandparents concerned about education, people who are caring for elderly parents, the shared support and information is nirvana.

In the cyber "room to work," we must be both technically and socially adept to manage our professional and personal success in the twenty-first century.

MINGLING BY MODEM

There are several methods of conversing online: chat rooms, forums, usenets and e-mail. While e-mail is the "least sexy" usage, according to *The Wall Street Journal*'s Walter Mossberg, it is the "most compelling, addictive and practical activity available online."

From babies to bubbas to boomers to bubbes . . . everybody's doin' it! Four hundred million e-mail boxes in the first quarter of 1999 proves that we are connecting in cyberspace in astronomical numbers. It leaves a lot of opportunity for errors.

Virtual communication has a history but was mostly used three and a half decades ago by the military, the government and academia. Now it is de rigueur. While some business owners don't seem to think it's a necessary tool, most businesses and companies in the year 2000 understand that customer service includes communication options.

While some days I feel like sending a fax or picking up the phone to hear the person's voice (these days, that is mostly to leave a message), the option of writing an e-mail at 11:30 P.M. is great. Whether it is to my best friend in Boston or my editor in New York, in the morning (when I am still asleep) when they log on, there I am . . . or, at least my message. Managing our actions and behaviors in the virtual room is as important as how we behave in the "real" rooms we visit.

Recent research out of Stanford University is that time spent on the Internet is causing Americans to "spend less time with friends and family," according to

Norman Nie, a political scientist. Yet we still have to know *how* to work virtual rooms as well as how often.

INSTANT MESSAGE MADNESS

When we "work" the virtual room or are logged on, we can learn if our "buddies" are online, too. We can say hello and have a side-bar chat that resembles a real conversation (except there is nothing visual or auditory to act as clues).

However, sometimes the instant message is an interference and brings another line of behaviors into question. Susan Sikora, a San Francisco talk-show host, wondered, "What if I am working on a project? or a deadline? Do I answer or ignore? How do I 'bow out' graciously if it is an inconvenient time for me to chat? And the 'handle' . . . what if I don't recognize the clever-masked name?"

Let common sense be the guide. If you have the time for an instant conversation, you'll know. If you want to respond and then go back to work, say so. "So glad to hear from you. Working on a deadline. Hope all is well. Take care (or Good-bye)." Or do what many people do, just ignore the instant message. That may be rude to some, but others find that being engaged in a side conversation in a chat room or while online is annoying and disruptive.

BREVITY? THE SOUL OF WIT OR WITLESS!

I have read a number of e-mail do's and don'ts lists in the last decade since I wrote one that was published in 1993 in *The Secrets of Savvy Networking*. Flipping through my own book and finding this list totally surprised, and pleased, me. I had forgotten that I had written it!

So many lists admonish e-mailers to "keep it brief." *That can be good advice, some of the time.* If by brief we are thinking telegram-like staccato word use, as if we paid by the letter, let's rethink that.

Including a pleasantry, a greeting, an appropriate "please" or "thank you" or a personable p.s. adds the high touch to our high-tech touching base.

WARNING: When we count our words, we may be discounting our message. Strike a balance between long and terse. As a former English major and teacher, I would summarize by saying that *we can have short sentences, just not sound "short" in our sentences. We want them to be declarative (statements) not imperative (orders).*

Example:

A. "Joe, it would help if you could get us the figures by today. Thanks."
B. "Get us the figures by today."

To which one would you be inclined to respond? If you read these samples and think B is correct "because it's to the point and doesn't waste words and time," please visit my website (www.susanroane.com) and take my "Schmooze Quotient Quiz" (see Glossary).

THE LEVEL PLAYING FIELD

One of the advantages and a great beauty of virtual communication is that our physical attributes have no bearing on what we "say" and no effect on others. I can remember an e-mail exchange with someone who had read *What Do I Say Next?* where I reveled in the equality of the virtual room.

She was hearing-impaired and shared with me just how e-mail and usenet groups and its variations allowed her to be more effective, successful and confident. And she was not judged or embarrassed by the comment, joke or directive she could not fully and accurately hear! For me, someone who taught school with the hearing-impaired, and learned some signing, that e-mail went to my heart.

A CHAT ROOM CHALLENGE

People in online communities often have "Net get-togethers." We want to meet our friends, new pals and supporters, but "we have expectations based on our online interactions," according to Red Dana. Her online group met for "beverages" in San Francisco's multimedia gulch. "One of the guys was so witty and clever in our chat room. But at our gathering he seemed very aloof and withdrawn. Halfway through the evening we finally learned he had hearing loss. And we were not facing him when we spoke! Once we finally learned that news, we changed our positions and he was part of the conversation."

Chat rooms enhance professional connections and e-mail allows us to "do our business" and stay in touch with friends and family. Beverly Borok, a Silicon Valley medical technologist, found that the opportunity to e-mail her son, Aron, propelled her into the online world. He was stationed in Siberia with the Peace Corps and other means of conversation were difficult, if not impossible.

E-MAILSTROM

Some of us "work" the virtual room all the time! I first read about Dr. Kimberly Young's online-addiction research in 1995 and now almost five years later, I am convinced that over 60 percent of the wired would answer yes to most of her questions.

**Signs You May Be Hooked
A Quick Quiz**

- Do you compulsively check your e-mail (ten to twenty times a day)?
- Do you lose track of time when you are online?
- Are you experiencing a problem in personal relations that can be blamed on the time you spend online?
- Have you gained weight or suffered eye, neck or back strain from hours online?

If you answered yes to any of these questions, log off— go to a movie, take a walk, meet a friend for latté or read a book! Now, that's a thought. . . .

FAMILY INTER(NET)VENTION

A colleague complained bitterly about a cousin who has used cyberspace for her own (mis)conception of the "Cousins Club." "She sends ten 'FWD' e-mails a week of jokes, poignant poetry (to her) and other drivel. There is never a 'Hello. How are you?' just her FWD e-mails with the six screens of recipients. If she was so adept at using her computer, she could at least 'cut and paste' and send just the message, with a one-sentence note. If there were techno-torture chambers, we'd put her in one!" My friend said that it did bring the cousins closer together and increased communication about how to stop this very "FWD" person.

A LIGHT-HEARTED LOOK AT SCREEN GEMS

My brother, Ira, has a differing view. "I like to see who else is on the list and where I ranked. My friend's father sent an e-mail and I was number three on the list; she was number ten! It was so much fun to call and give her a good-natured raze on her ranking!"

Ira must not be the only person who checks lists, as I received an e-mail from a long-lost acquaintance because she saw SusanRoAne@aol.com on someone's group e-mail list. Now that is another "way to work" the virtual world!

If cousins get riled at numerous, blanketed, forwarded e-mails, you can imagine what colleagues think of it—or us! We all have people who have added our names to lists on which we did not want our names. And we want off and out!

WHAT TO SAY TO A "FWD" PERSON

We can delete . . . and/or say something to the sender. I had to say something to a friend/colleague and said it in a real-time conversation so that my tone, my pacing and my sincerity and caring could be heard:

"I really enjoy hearing from you, but I don't read FWDed online jokes, especially if there is more than one screen of names. I would much prefer just hearing from you and how you are, and am so glad you stay in touch."

We are still friends, and do business by phone, in person and online.

HOW NOT TO BE "MO-DUMB"

The cyber room is unstructured and yet, as there has always been throughout history, there is a codification of the laws. While Moses did not bring the cyber laws down from the Mount Sinai of Modems ("Take two tablets and e-mail me in the morning"), they rule! And, so do the courts!

E-mails on company time can be used against us. The *New York Times* recently fired employees for the cyber passing of an inappropriate e-mail (1999). And before we hit the send button, we need to reread our e-mails to be sure they *should* be sent, and that we are sending them only to those intended to read them.

Companies are now buying computer programs to monitor employee use and abuse of company time for employees' computer use.

BE AWARE: The programs can reconstruct e-mails, letter by keystroke.

THE UNBEARABLE "LITE"NESS OF BEING—
SELF-ABSORBED

Seth Godin wrote the book *Permission Marketing* and it makes sense. Before he did, people with (cyber) sense knew not to send "stuff" without permission. In the old days, when it existed, it was called common sense, common courtesy and good business.

An author who wanted my feedback on his book really broke these rules on several counts. He sent me a 119-page e-mailed document (281 kilobytes)! I was appalled. He "screwed up" because he never asked me:

- if I was interested in seeing it,
- if I had time to sit in front of a screen to read, assess and edit it,
- if I would waste my computer time printing it,
- if this fell under the guidelines for Pick My Brain Consulting, where I coach would-be authors.

He supposed I would do this for him in my "spare" time—when I am not writing books, giving speeches, running my business, working out, doing my charity work, hanging out with my friends and family or doing the laundry! (Notice which is last on my list.)

Getting permission is important and can enhance business success. Not everyone who gives you a business card at an event wants to receive your weekly e-mailed missives, sales pitches or recirculated jokes.

MIXED AND MANGLED MESSAGES

Chat rooms are about conversation, exchanges of information, thoughts, ideas, helpful hints, stats, good news and laughter. E-mail is the same. It is also about conversation, although asynchronistic. It can, in the best of worlds, be a version of that wonderful, almost lost art form, the letter!

Last holiday season, the last of the twentieth century, felt very special. When I saw "Holiday Greetings" from a colleague I liked, I opened it . . . even knowing it was a generic message. Generic I could handle. What I read was indefensible. Under the guise of holiday blessings was a blatant sales pitch for her books, audiotapes and newest workshop for which we could register (and pay).

"Miss Holiday Greeting" may receive her desired response among those who need her "instructions." But to those of us who fancied ourselves colleagues, buddies and classy enough not to confuse and abuse Christmas with crassness, we were offended!

Sending a mixed marketing message under the heading of "blessings" could create bad buzz on the World Wide Web and lose a friend. We should not OVERwork any room, cyber or real.

CAN WE *NOT* TALK?

There is a difference between those who prefer not talking to others and those who don't prefer it. There are times when it is appropriate and expedient to send the e-mail that confirms the meeting location or time. If it is important, we just have to be sure the e-mail is received.

Carl LaMell, president/CEO of Clearbrook, a non-profit organization that assists people with disabilities in the Chicago suburbs, called an urgent meeting of his senior staff . . . via e-mail. By coincidence, one of his directors called him about another issue. "We talked briefly and I closed with 'I'll see you later today at the meeting.' She sounded confused and asked me what I was talking about. She never received the e-mail. Now, we make sure there are voicemail confirmations as well."

The social or personal e-mail can also get lost in cyber-space. Before we get upset at the lack of response, resend it. Or at least ask if the e-mail arrived. A "gentleman caller" often e-mailed me about our "hooking up." One day he called to find out why I had not responded to his e-mail. He thought I had a change of heart and was just ignoring him. Not true. Fortunately, he called and we made our plans.

YOU'RE SUCH AN E-CARD—A CYBER "HALLMARK" OF DISTINCTION

The World Wide Web now provides us with greeting-card sites. They are fast, convenient, acknowledging—or are they? What they are is free. But not free from some issues and annoyances.

They often come with ads. And, according to Letitia Baldrige, etiquette expert, if the recipient must stop work to download the greeting "it's unpardonable." Another thought is that while e-greetings are convenient, they are a lazy way to remember an occasion. It's a way for the person who forgot—until that day—to show they were thinking of us. Yet, for those living in other parts of the world, it is the perfect option to stay in touch on important occasions without the global postal issues.

The birthday, Valentine's Day and holiday cards that I receive, read and display on my parson's table are now even more special. When it was time to change from Hanukkah, I reread my cards and saved them. Up went the birthday cards. When it was time to display Christmas cards, I reread the lovely thoughts, fun greetings, and birthday wishes of my friends . . . who "cared enough to send the very best." I, for one, will continue to buy, save and send real-time cards. It's the personal touch that cannot be replaced by cyber-sentiments.

THE E-NOTE OF THANKS

The perils of losing our personal touch are huge. It is perfectly sensible to dash off an e-thank-you note for a speedy acknowledgment. *(Then it is followed by the formal thank-you note.)* Are you cringing at the thought, because you are too busy to pick up a pen? Miss Manners and I have said that, if we have the time to unwrap, deposit, ingest, enjoy, wear and utilize "gifts," we certainly have the time to show our appreciation, manners and character by picking up a pen and writing a sentence or two. But if we are so busy that we cannot send a note, in the case of gifts, "send them back *unopened.*"

THE GIFT OF TIME, LEADS, INFORMATION, SUPPORT

The savvy networker also acknowledges the gifts we receive that are not wrapped and beribboned. We may shoot a quick e-mail to thank a colleague for a lead or a bit of helpful information. But then a note (handwritten, of course) is to follow. If the lead we get turns into a major client or a new job, the acknowledgment card should accompany a gift of thanks. Our behaviors distinguish ourselves from the crowd, and make us memorable. Let it be for the right reasons.

THE ONLINE "PEN" PAL

In some cases, our source of assistance who gave us the "gift" is known only by an online name. And we have no other information! Here's a concept—ask for a mailing address. If your cyber pal gave you a lead to a new client, job or solution to a problem, there must be enough trust so that asking for a mailing address would be appropriate.

SRoane@aol.com had received e-mails for me (SRoAne2224@aol.com). This nice man found me and forwarded my e-mails. We struck up an e-mail friendship, and I was just so taken with the fact that he was so kind to take the time to find me. He knew I was an author and a professional speaker as his wife had heard of my books and me. So, when they were expecting their first child, he let me know. When daughter Morgan was born, I asked him for his mailing address. Not to be invasive, but I had seen the cutest stuffed pink elephant and wanted to send it to her . . . as my way of thanking her dad. Infant son Joshua received a hat and matching booties . . . in blue!

When I was giving a presentation in Washington, D.C., several years ago, Stephen Roane, my e-mail pal, and I met for coffee, over pictures of Morgan, of course. We continue to stay in touch.

BREAKING UP IS HARD TO DO . . . IN PERSON

An associate of mine was one of the first of our crowd to experience a new low in cyber communication: the E-Mail Dump! Sounds like a perfect Seinfeld episode in which George or Elaine has the girl (boy) friend who is such a computer geek that she/he sends the "buzz off" by e-mail.

No, this actually happened. The "perp" was your basic Silicon Valley Boy, who often told her, "Some things are just not e-mails; they are conversations." Talk about words NOT matching behaviors!

Then, in 1999, e-mail breakups made front-page news in *The Wall Street Journal,* and the term "cyber jerk" was born. In February 2000, *The Wall Street Journal* reported the use by younger managers of e-mail as a firing tool. The person who has bad news to deliver, be it a downsizing, the loss of a loved one, a catastrophe . . . take heed. *Do NOT fire, quit nor dump via e-mail.*

Three Cs to Seize the Moment

When it involves another person, have the *courage,
consideration and character* to do what is difficult.
Face the music, face the person.

Because e-mail is easy to use, it does not mean that it
should be! Our behaviors are judged and remembered.
Some things merit conversation, not an e-mail.

A CONDOLENCE E-CARD?

If someone experiences the loss of a loved one, an e-mail
of support, sympathy and caring may be okay if it fits the
schematic of the online relationship.

And then the sympathy card or note is to follow. Like
other cards, they can be reread, held, displayed, reread
again, saved. Yes, an e-mail or e-card can be saved, but
there is no comparison. In this instance, a sympathy note
and/or card sustains the person in mourning. On the
printed card we send, a note in our own writing gives
comfort during a time of loss and grief. And, by the way,
expressing sympathy is best done in person or on the
phone, if distance is an issue.

In the case of it being a chat room– or online-only
pal who suffered a personal loss, online support and
expressions of condolence are okay.

There are rituals observed by people of different faiths.
Whether it is a wake, a funeral mass, a life celebration or

visiting a house of shivah (see Glossary), we want to be sure that we know the customs of that "room." For some, a flower wreath at the church service is appropriate. Other families prefer a donation to a nonprofit charity.

In this virtual room and world, there are still some situations that are not best served by anonymity and speed. We are judged by our behaviors in virtual and "real" rooms and want to avoid being characterized as sleazes.

ROANE'S REMINDERS

Do

- Proofread for punctuation, spelling and flow (but grammar- and spell-check are not sufficient).
- Check your e-mail regularly, and if you do so more than eight times a day, take the Addiction Quiz (see page 49).
- Remember the "magic" words and pleasantries.
- Assess the situations that require real time communication, even if e-mail is easier.

Don't

- Use obscenities. They read worse than they sound.
- Send more than one screen of information without permission.
- Fire, dump or reprimand.
- Use all uppercase letters . . . it is shouting.
- Send any mail you would not want to be read by others, in public or in court!
- Use your office computer for relaying jokes/messages that could cost you your job.
- Forward screens of e-mail sayings, jokes, warnings.
- Waste people's e-time.
- Send an e-mail written in anger (wait a day, reread, reassess).

6

MR. (OR MS.) SLEAZE WORKS A ROOM: OR HOW *NOT* TO DO IT

The people who are the most successful at working a room are those who genuinely like, respect and trust other people. When we don't really care about other people, they sense the insincerity and rarely take kindly to it. Both my readers and audience members, from CPAs to CEOs, have shared horrifying stories about the smarmy and ill-behaved bulldozers who may even think they are creating rapport!

BEING "SLIMED"

At a benefit, Richard, who was very involved in politics, approached me and told me that he "*really* knew how to work a room" and "had a great deal of experience at it." He appeared to be knowledgeable, charming and smooth— on the surface. But as we spoke, *his eyes moved around the room to see who else was there,* and I sensed he wasn't about to waste time with people he didn't consider important. He had no idea how to manage his mingling!

Richard personified the recent results of research from Dr. David Dunning of Cornell University, that the "incompetent are often supremely confident of their abilities. They are blissfully ignorant, because the skills required for competent assessment are also the ones they are missing."

Everything Richard did seemed calculated. He heard my words and responded, but he didn't really listen. When *he* spoke—mostly about himself, his past, his ideas, his successes, his goals—he locked me in with eyes that felt like lasers.

Like Bill Murray in *Ghostbusters,* I felt like I'd been "slimed"! Mr. Sleaze was a user and a loser. And, unfortunately, he's still on the loose. We see sleazes at networking events, association gatherings, even at church and synagogue functions. They overwork a room and are to be avoided and never emulated.

> *Top Tip: If you can tell someone is*
> *WORKING a room, that person is doing*
> *it wrong!*

MR. OR MS. SLEAZE'S DISGUISES

We've all met the Sleazes at parties, meetings and conferences. They may wear two-thousand-dollar Brioni or Chanel suits instead of the proverbial "sharkskin." They

© Chronicle Features, 1988

Mr. Lapham is going to be our sleaze factor.

may look perfectly conservative and stylish. They may even appear to be the Prince or Princess of our personal or professional dreams. And they may say all the right things.

But you just *know* they don't really care about you, your latest microchip design, your dotcom IPO, or your career or anything that isn't about them. They almost never follow through with what they promise.

Their behaviors do not support their words. If our behavior does not support our words, it subverts them. And we are remembered for bad behavior.

The Sleazes of the world come in many forms. They

are male and female, techies or Luddites, young, old and middle-aged, wealthy and struggling. They can be anyone. The common denominator: They have no respect for anyone who can't "do something for them." They are just trying to make their *contact quota*, and it shows. And that is *not* how we make contacts that create connections with colleagues, coworkers, clients and cronies. They think networking and mingling are sciences that can be quantified. No, they are the ART of communication.

LEARNING FROM SLEAZE

Is there a lesson in Mr. or Ms. Sleaze's behavior? You bet. **The technical skills of working a room are not enough;** the warmth and desire to help others must be genuine and sincere.

I hate to sound like Grandma, but when in doubt, apply the Golden Rule. Treat other people as you would want to be treated. It's old-fashioned, but it's easy, true and almost fail-safe. Dr. Tony Alessandra, author of *The Platinum Rule,* recommends we go a step farther and observe people's behavior and treat them as they want to be treated.

I say "almost" fail-safe because there are some people—only a few, fortunately—who don't care how we treat them, because they don't care about *us.* They treat everyone with a chilling combination of disregard and disdain, and don't expect anything different from others. They are the roadblock number 4 people who tempt us to not Risk Rejection. All you can do is apply remedy number 4 and move on.

NO JOKING MATTER—HUMOR THAT HURTS

The jokester who works a room with inappropriate humor has the same effect as insect repellent. We need to be sure we do not comment on something that could embarrass another person—something the latter can't change overnight.

The Humor Library in San Francisco contains most of the research studies on humor. That is where my suspicions of gender differences in humor were confirmed. Males generally found the teasing/poking-fun humor to be funny, while women preferred situational humor. Think twice before saying "that funny thing" if it is at someone else's expense. My mother's warning applies: "Listen to what people say when they are joking; much truth is said in jest."

FATAL FLAWS

There is good news and bad news for Mr. and Ms. Sleaze. The good news is that if being remembered is the goal, they achieve it. People do remember. And it can get you "discussed."

The bad news is that they are remembered for all the wrong reasons. The Sleazes leave a negative impression, and that rarely enhances one's social life or business network.

In addition to being remembered as an insincere user and an unfeeling manipulator, Mr. or Ms. Sleaze often brings to the meeting or party a whole bag of unpleasant social "tricks."

Avoid all of these behaviors and the people who exhibit them!

HOW TO HANDLE A SLEAZE

Extricate yourself . . . quickly. There is no reason for you to put up with this kind of behavior or to waste your time being gracious to someone who doesn't even know or care that you are being gracious. Try to be polite, but remember that a Sleaze isn't terribly sensitive to the difference between polite and impolite. Dr. Dunning's research about the incompetent rings true here. The most important thing is to get away. Excuse yourself and get away by saying, "Oh, I hope you enjoy the rest of the event." Then move at least one quarter of the room away. If the person committed an unpardonable act, just excuse yourself and move on.

ROANE'S REMINDERS

Sleazes come in a variety of disguises and tend to

- make others uncomfortable
- be self-absorbed
- look past you to see who else is in the room
- try to push their agenda, products or services
- drink too much
- tell off-color, inappropriate jokes
- have no interest in those who can't help them
- try to make their contract quota
- make fun of others as a "conversation ploy"
- size up people based on "titles"

If you have met a sleaze, the voice in your stomach will signal you clearly. Pay attention and MOVE ON!

☺ GET SET! ☺

SEVEN STEPS FOR PLANNING YOUR PRESENCE: PREPARATION

You're set to go! You've identified the roadblocks, applied the remedies, seen the specific benefits of working a room, polished up your chutzpah and your charm and learned to avoid either resembling or spending time with Mr. or Ms. Sleaze.

What's next? Before you rush out into the night, or the afternoon, or the morning—take some time to PRE-PARE yourself.

The old army saw about the five Ps also holds true for business and social events: PRIOR PLANNING PRE-VENTS POOR PERFORMANCE.

Whether the event is a cocktail party, a political fund-raiser, a dinner meeting, a conference or a reunion, *be prepared.*

You have to do your homework. You have to know what the event is, who is sponsoring it, who will attend and think of what *you* have in common with *them.* Before you leave for any event, be sure to check your business-card case, your grooming, and these seven steps.

1. ADOPT A POSITIVE ATTITUDE

Your attitude can make the difference between an event that is pleasant and successful—and one that ranks with the sinking of the *Titanic* (not the movie!). Unless you've been blessed (or cursed) with a poker face, it is extremely difficult to mask a negative attitude.

If you go to an event thinking, "Well, I have to be here but I just know I'm going to have a bad time," trust me, you will! If you don't want to be "there," people will know it.

If for some reason you really don't want to go to an event, then DON'T. Better not to go than to create a lasting, lousy impression.

You owe it to yourself to satisfy your own needs first, and the fact that you don't want or need to be there will show on your face. Even if you plaster on a smile, *it will show in your eyes.*

Why waste a new shirt or a freshly-cleaned silk dress or the *time* it takes to attend an event if you don't plan to enjoy yourself?

The only people who consistently go to events intending to have a bad time are those who suffer from what I call the "Lemon Sucker Syndrome."

You can identify these people by the look on their faces—*excruciating pain,* for no apparent reason. Lemon Suckers are miserable, and they *love* their misery! If you try to cheer them up, they'll hate you for it. You may have a Lemon Sucker in your office or in your family.

Even those of us who are not Lemon Suckers can occasionally *look* that way unless we prepare a positive attitude before the event. And most people have enough experience with the Lemon-Sucker Syndrome that they will give us a wide berth if they see that uninviting look.

We check our makeup and straighten our ties before going out. A positive attitude is even more important, and deserves at least as much attention. I'm not saying you have to bubble like a high school cheerleader in order to appear upbeat, pleasant and positive. A little bit of enthusiasm and a smile go a long way.

The best way I know to generate enthusiasm, if it is not already there, involves step number two.

2. FOCUS ON THE BENEFITS OF THE EVENT

In chapter 3, we discussed the importance of knowing WHY you are attending a meeting, party, dinner or reception. The twenty-first century finds us with many tugs for our time, so you must know what you stand to gain from leaving your home or office and working the room. Your goals, which will vary from event to event, will keep you on track.

Is your purpose in attending this event to be visible among your peers? To show the boss that you support her favorite community project? To be a role model for your employees and demonstrate the importance of participating in the trade association?

I attend events sponsored by my local chamber of commerce and by the convention and visitors bureau in order to stay visible and reconnect with my business buddies. My purpose is not to sell books or book speaking engagements, but to touch base with my business and social networks and to have fun. Business may follow . . . or may not—but staying visible is important.

It is perfectly acceptable to attend an event because you "have to"—as long as you've prepared a positive attitude. Whether you are in Generation X, Y or "Me," the purpose of going to an event may be that "duty calls." Just as on Mother's Day and Thanksgiving, there are certain events where our presence is expected, and the goal may be to fulfill this obligation.

That doesn't mean you have to have a bad time. Even if you "have to" attend a certain cocktail party, you can also focus on the benefits of meeting new people, exchanging conversation and bringing back some business cards to expand your network. And having fun!

Before the event, take some time to fill out an index card like this one. If you find that your list of benefits continues on the back of the card, so much the better!

EVENT :	LOCATION:
SPONSOR:	ATTENDEES:
Benefits of Participation	
Professional	Personal

You might even slip the card into your purse or wallet, re-create it on your PDA (personal digital assistant) and sneak a look at it before you enter the room. It will remind you of your focus, and of how you are being compensated for your time—in nonmonetary and perhaps even monetary terms.

> *A WORD OF CAUTION: Be* **guided** *by your goals, not* **blinded** *by them.*

We all know people who are on their way to their goals, and watch out for anyone who gets in their way! These people don't usually attract others to them or work a room with much success. Their charm level is nonexistent, and they are transparent.

Focusing on the benefits of an event helps generate enthusiasm and keeps us on track, but genuine warmth and interest in other people are what make us succeed.

3. PLAN YOUR SELF-INTRODUCTION

The best self-introductions are energetic and pithy—no more than seven to nine seconds long. They include your name (obviously) and a tag line that tells other people who you are and gives them a way to remember you. Giving a benefit of what you do gives other people the opportunity to relate, ask a question or share an observation.

Have different self-introductions for different events.

John Doe, the new director of development for Memorial Hospital, might use these variations:

- At his first meeting of the Development Directors' Association, where everyone in attendance is a director of development, he might say, "I'm the money-raiser for Memorial." It's alliterative and memorable.

- At a cocktail party to introduce administrators to new board members, he would say, "I'm John Doe, your director of development."

- At his daughter's wedding, "I'm John Doe, Mary's father." Or more lightly, "I'm providing the dough for this party."

These introductions are pretty basic. It helps to include a little humor. At the introductory meeting of a nonsmoking seminar, John might say something like, "I'm John Doe, and I consider myself this program's greatest challenge."

Your self-introduction has three purposes: (1) to tell people who you are, (2) to give them a pleasant experience of you and (3) to give them a way to engage.

Speak clearly and *look people in the eye.* Your introduction can be laced with humor and perhaps even some information that will stimulate conversation. But in the final analysis, *what people will remember is the warmth and enthusiasm they feel from you.*

4. CHECK YOUR BUSINESS CARDS

Before there were business cards, there were calling cards, and their function was similar. Handing out business cards tells people your name, company and position, and gives them a way to contact you in the future.

Some people take business cards for granted. They grab a fistful before leaving their home or office, give some out if others happen to ask for them, and collect other people's cards, which then end up at the bottom of

their purses or in the deep recesses of their wallets. Some time later (a week to three years) and for whatever reason (usually a new purse or wallet), these potentially valuable resources surface—dog-eared and well on their way to biodegrading from a visit to the cleaners.

This is not the purpose of business cards. The purpose of business cards is to give people a tangible, physical way to remember you and something they can slip directly into their card files or scan into their contact-management programs. This is also how you should use *other* people's cards.

GUIDELINES FOR BUSINESS CARDS

- *Make sure that your name, your company name and your numbers are readable.* Select a typeface that is big enough and clear enough so that no one needs a magnifying glass or four-foot arms to read your card. Fold-over cards do not work in a Rolodex. Neither do vertical cards. Forget the fancy designs that obscure the numbers. Place your phone number last, after your fax number. E-mail addresses should be easy to read. Website addresses should be in a bold typeface to stand out.

- *Devise a system for carrying your own cards and for collecting cards from others.* I use a large cigarette case, with a baseball card to divide my cards from those I've collected.

  If you are comfortable with using a computer to organize the cards when you get back to your home or office, by all means do so. If you are part of the Not Yet Computer Literate Set, as I am, clip the cards together by event and date. That way you can reach into your business-card file box and—once you remember the event—you're home free.

Filing a card is helpful only if you can retrieve it by remembering the person's name and why you wanted to contact that particular person. The next tip will help you remember.

- *Write a mnemonic device on the other person's card*—as soon as possible—to help you remember who they are. If you plan on scanning the card, do not write on the front of it.

- *Bring enough cards.* I learned from my "femtor," the late Sally Livingston, that no one wanted to take home a used napkin—even if it had my name and number on it. Napkins don't fit into anyone's Rolodex. The excuse that "I just gave out my last card" is questionable and smacks of poor planning. No one is impressed by how many people we met moving down the buffet from the brie to the meatballs.

- *Never leave home without them!* As Mom says, "You never know who you'll run into." I keep business cards in the pocket of my running suit!

- *Do NOT pass out brochures.* Brochures are expensive. They are meant for people who are genuinely inter-ested in doing business with you. They are also bulky. People at a reception have no place to put them, and nobody wants to leave looking like they should have brought a shopping cart. Brochures are also a great way to follow up, so don't waste that opportunity by giving them away at the first meeting.

- *If you want to give your card to someone but they have not asked for it, ask for theirs first.* "May I have your card?" Most people will respond in kind, especially if you hold your own card conspicuously, as if you are ready to trade. "May I offer you my card?" is clear and polite.

- *Avoid "sticky" situations.* Don't reach for the buffet with one hand and your card with the other. No one wants to take home a card caked with sweet and sour sauce.

- *Pass out your cards selectively.* If your gut gives you a warning, heed it. Don't use business cards to play power games. Not everyone should have your business card. Keep your own safety and sanity in mind. *The exchange of cards should follow a conversation in which rapport has been established.* Don't give them to people in whom you can barely detect a pulse. Ask yourself if you actually want this person to call you. Above all, be protective and polite.

Let's borrow from the Japanese tradition: When you receive a card, *honor* it by looking at it, looking at the person. Perhaps you can make a comment about the card. That focus helps you remember people. In *The Secrets of Savvy Networking,* I expanded these tips into a chapter.

If your company does not provide you with a card, have one made at your local instant printer so you can help people remember you.

5. PREPARE YOUR SMALL TALK

Some people cringe at this idea. They don't like the notion of preparing conversation, and they say that small talk is trivial. I say, "How do you start a conversation with a stranger? With war? Famine? Floods?" Hardly.

Whether the event is social or professional, there may be no special host to ease you into the room and help begin conversations. You may be on your own.

Small talk allows you to learn about other people. If you think about what has been said and respond to that, you're communicating. Small talk is absolutely essential; it is a way of finding mutual areas of interest. In *What Do I Say Next?* I wrote that small talk equals big business, and it does.

SILENCE IS NOT GOLDEN

In *The Art of Conversation,* James Morris points out that although we "realize that it is bad manners to monopolize a conversation, it's equally bad manners not to talk enough."

One of my favorite authors, Michael Korda, author of *Success, Power and Queenie and Another Life,* is the nephew of movie magnate Sir Alexander Korda. Korda says that one of the things his uncle had going for him was that he never let things get *too serious.* In an article on small talk in *Signature* (September 1986) Korda says, "A bore is someone who has no small talk. . . . Silence is not golden—it is the kiss of death."

In this same article, Korda discusses the difference between small talk and large talk: "Large talk is for business negotiations, medical matters, things that involve money, health, life, the law. . . . *Small talk should intrigue, delight, amuse, fill up time pleasantly.* Given that, anything will do, from dogs to delicatessens. The aim of small talk is to make people comfortable—to put them at their ease—not to teach, preach or impress. It's a game, like tennis, in which the object is to keep the ball in the air for as long as possible."

You will walk into a room with more confidence if you have at least three pieces of small talk prepared—light conversations that you can have with anyone you meet. Whether it's mother boards, mother ships or motherhood, an exchange of pleasantries makes everyone feel more comfortable before you begin to think on your feet.

Bring your OAR: Observe, Ask, Reveal. The topics might include a local sports team, the organization for which you are meeting or even the weather! You will have *something* in common with these people, simply because you are attending the same event. It's best to avoid controversial subjects like politics and religion, but you will probably find several areas of common interest if you look. Dan Maddux, executive director of the American Payroll Association, recommends that his staff read *People* magazine. "It's a great source of conversational tidbits, fills you in on what's going on and is generally *not* controversial!"

> *Being a good conversationalist includes being a good listener. When people talk about themselves, listen with your ears, with your* face *and with your heart.*

Conversations are best when *both* people try to find common areas, are genuinely interested in one another and contribute. Remember: *The* banquet of banter is a potluck.

Serious discussions have their place, and you may enjoy deep, intimate talk with your friends. Probing conversations are off-putting. Small talk is a good way to break the ice and *begin* friendships.

More later in chapter 8 about starting, continuing and ending conversations.

6. REMEMBER TO MAKE EYE CONTACT AND SMILE

"It's good to meet you" is only believable if your voice, tone and warm, sincere smile match your words. This line doesn't play very well through a frown, or even through a look of indifference.

Eye contact and being in the moment are critical in building rapport. A colleague and his wife attended a birthday party for one of her associates. My friend told me later that the "birthday boy," a middle manager for a bank, never looked him in the eye as he shook his hand. "He all but said, 'I'm looking for someone more important to talk to,'" my colleague said. "I was ticked off. How did he know I wasn't more important—or would be someday?"

A roving eye gives the impression of an insincere, hand-pumping Mr. Sleaze. People always remember the room surfer.

But a word of caution. . . . Eye contact does not mean *glaring* or *staring,* which can be rude. Glaring rarely builds rapport or enhances communication. Author David Givens suggests that we alternate between looking at the person and looking away in order to display just enough interest, and also just enough vulnerability to be approached. "Cultural standards vary, but in the United States a comfortable range is looking for seven seconds, and then looking away for only a few seconds." Beyond that, the "looking" may become a glare or the "looking away" may suggest that we're scanning the room for better opportunities.

7. PRACTICE YOUR HANDSHAKE

A handshake is the business greeting in America. Jellyfish need not apply here. A firm clasp is the handshake of preference for *greeting* people, *agreeing* to a deal and *departing* as friends. It's a web-to-web handshake that is neither weak nor forceful. We want to be mindful of arthritis, and the rise of carpal tunnel syndrome.

These are some handshakes to *avoid:*

- *The Jellyfish.* A limp hand moves your way. You grasp it and it turns to mush. Do you want to do business with this person? People with jellyfish handshakes create the impression that they are spineless—an unsavory perception, to be sure.

- *The Knuckle Breaker.* Your hand disappears into a vice and comes back the worse for wear. This kind of power play is best left to members of the Mafia. In recent years, some women have adopted the Knuckle

Breaker in an effort not to be perceived as pushovers. Women do need to have firm handshakes, but I recently met a young attorney who was five feet one, 103 pounds, and shook my hand with such strength that it came back feeling like chopped meat. At a seminar in Toronto, a fellow about six foot three responded to my handshake with such a knuckle— breaker that I screamed, "Ouch!" Was he trying to show me his strength or power? He showed me that he had no clue about handshakes.

- *The Finger Squeeze.* This person doesn't clasp your hand; he or she grabs your *fingers only.* When done with a light touch, this gesture appears prissy and/or suggests that the person isn't sure he wants to touch your *whole* hand. With a heavy touch, the Finger Squeeze can become the Ring Squeeze. Marks from your ring are clearly etched in at least two other fingers, and you wonder if you should leave the reception and get an X ray.

- *The Covered Handshake.* In this handshake, one of the parties puts his or her left hand over the hands clasped in the handshake. This may be perceived as a show of warmth by those of us who are "touchers." But others may see it as a power play or feel that they are being patronized.

  There may be times when a covered handshake is perfectly appropriate. Be sensitive to other people's responses, and let your intuition be your guide.

We don't want to become overly analytical. Several years ago, a Ford Fellow and I were doing some consulting on the same project. He pointed out that I touched people as I spoke, and very seriously told me that this was "a schematic organizational power play." That was what he did . . . plan power plays.

"How interesting," I replied. "And all this time I thought it was because I was from a long line of touchers!"

Since it's not always easy to read people or to assess their reaction to a covered handshake, play it safe and stick with the traditional firm clasp, with no left hand playing around the edges.

MEN, WOMEN AND HANDSHKES

Men have been trained from childhood to shake hands. Women must also master the art. It's up to the woman to *extend her hand first* whether she is meeting a man or another woman. Men are taught to wait and see if the woman initiates a handshake. A woman never conveys a mixed message by extending her hand to a man—unless, of course, she is wearing a see-through blouse!

THE BUSINESS KISS

To Miss Manners's horror, kissing has also become a business greeting in certain industries. "Bussing for business" is common in the entertainment, hospitality and human resource fields. People involved in banking, manufacturing, accounting and the law are less likely to be seen blowing one another little "air kisses." In the days of sexual harassment grievances and lawsuits, just be careful.

So, never in the office, and never on the mouth. A kiss is a feature of a relationship, a friendship, and is never to be presumed. It is safest to make do with a handshake; the only "kosher" (see Glossary) contact!

THE MICHAEL JORDAN "NO BULL" SOLUTION

If *you* are uncomfortable and want to avoid the kiss as a business greeting, simply stand as far away from the other person as the length of your arm. Extend your hand, *smile* and **lock your elbow.** If Michael did this, he would keep people about five feet away from him. It's a good way to give yourself some "breathing space" and still make others feel welcome.

ANOTHER "TOUCHY" SUBJECT

Being a "breath of fresh air" at every meeting, interview and party is the optimum behavior. To that end, you may want to avoid garlic and onions before any event. And carry mints . . . to enhance your well-minted mingling.

A word to the wise: Observe people's behaviors—their facial expressions, gestures and body language. While it is *not* a quantifiable science, there is a great deal of information—books and websites—on the subject of body language that is useful.

ROANE'S REMINDERS

Take the time to "be prepared." Remember the seven steps for planning your presence:

1. Adopt a positive attitude.
2. Focus on the benefits of the event.
3. Plan your self-introduction.
4. Check your business cards.
5. Prepare your small talk. Bring your O.A.R. (Observe, Ask, Reveal).
6. Remember to make eye contact and smile.
7. Practice your handshake.

Advisories:

- Kiss off the kissing.
- Be conscious of body language.
- Avoid garlic and onions.
- Have fun and the room will "work" you!

8

SEVEN STRATEGIES: FROM JUMP START TO SMOOTH STOP

You've done your preparation, but what if your internal engine starts to stall at the thought of actually walking in the door? These seven strategies will give you a quick jump start and bring you through the event to a smooth stop.

1. THE ENTRANCE: GRAND OR OTHERWISE

What time should you arrive? Arrival time is usually based on the starting time of the event—not on making a conspicuous entrance. There is no such thing as being "fashionably late" to a meeting. Take a tip from shy people: They arrive on time or within fifteen minutes of the appointed hour. That's how they avoid walking into a crowded room.

When you arrive at the event, take a deep breath, stand tall and walk *into* the room. Hanging out in the doorway creates a fire hazard, a traffic problem and the impression that you're either timid about coming in or are standoffish.

There may or may not be an official greeter. Antici-
pate that there will *not* be one, and enjoy the pleasant
surprise if there is.

Speaker and author Judith Briles recommends volunteering to be on the greeting committee yourself. That
way "you get to meet everyone because it's your job." If
you are shy, this gives you something to say to people
right away.

Give the room a quick once-over. Where is the bar?
Where is the food? Where are people congregating? Where
can you position yourself to meet the most people?

A professional speaker who addresses audiences of
thousands once told me he had great difficulty attending
cocktail parties and talking to people one-to-one. His
solution is to position himself between the entry and the
buffet table so that everyone has to walk by him to get to
the food. He is always surrounded by people . . . albeit
hungry ones.

Once you are in the room, look around for people
you know. If you see someone who looks vaguely familiar, go up and introduce yourself. Find out if that person
is who you thought he or she was. There is no point in
wondering, "What would happen if . . ." One of two
things will happen: (1) You'll be right and renew the
acquaintance, or (2) You'll meet a new person. Chat for a
while and move on.

2. THE BUDDY SYSTEM

If the thought of entering a room gives you the shakes,
try the Buddy System. Make a deal with a friend who

must also attend these events, and go together. But don't limit your arrangement to "having someone with whom to walk in the door." The Buddy System can be a great way to work a room—if you do some prior planning and strategizing.

BUDDY STRATEGIES

- *One of the main advantages of going to an event with a buddy is that you can introduce each other around.* You may know people your buddy doesn't know, and vice versa. Even if neither of you knows *anyone,* you'll both meet people in the course of the event and can introduce each other to your *new* acquaintances.

  Brush up on your introduction skills so that you present your buddy as a pleasant, interesting person who has something in common with the other attendees. *This means listening to people to find out what their interests are.*

  Give people enough information about your buddy to begin a conversation, and use a positive tone of voice.

- *Make sure your buddy does the same.* Patricia Fripp and I do this at many events. She says, "It's like being with your own PR person. We say about each other that which we would *not* say about ourselves. 'Have you met Susan RoAne, best-selling author with over a million books in print and a great speaker?'" I introduce Patricia similarly. "Have you met Patricia Fripp, one of the best speakers in the country and an author as well?" Believe me, conversations happen!

Don Hansen, a Seattle-based business consultant, says that some people are "legitimizers" simply by virtue of who they are and how they introduce other people. They are individuals with a certain amount of status, and they *know how to present other people* in the *best light.* That is something we all can do.

- *You and your buddy will want to split up as soon as possible.* If you act like you are velcroed together, your ability to work the room and meet people is limited. (Most people will not approach two people, as it feels invasive.) You'll meet only half the number of people, and those you do meet will think you are joined at the hip. This also applies to significant others who can be "buddies." This is a terrific strategy for spouses. Meet and mingle separately and then reconnect.

- *Develop a "rescue" signal* so that you and your buddy can regroup to assess and restrategize, and help extricate one another from conversations that have gone on too long.

3. THE WHITE-KNUCKLED DRINKER—AND OTHER ACCESSIBLE FOLK

You're inside the room, and you and your buddy have decided it's time to split up. Where do you turn? Who do you talk to? You don't recognize a soul, and feel conspicuous standing alone. The temptation at this point is find a place near the wall and try to blend in.

Initiating conversation can be challenging. Remember, our mothers taught us *not* to talk to strangers. But we've remedied that. We also fear rejection, and perhaps suspect that we're not interesting, witty or attractive enough. But we've remedied those things, too. And because we are attending this reception in order to meet others, *we can't afford to be wallflowers.* It's time to step out there on our own, work up our courage and *do something.*

What I do in this situation is look for the "white-knuckled" drinkers. If you want to manage the mingling at any event, look for people who are standing around with their cup or glass of wine, coffee or water, clutching it so tightly that their knuckles are taut. They are more uncomfortable that we are, probably shyer and just as interesting.

These people usually welcome your conversation because you save them from anonymity. No one else is talking to them. If you walk up and start a conversation, you're doing a good deed, earning a few "Planet Points"™ and also moving *yourself* away from the wall. ("Planet Points" are what we get for earning our right on the planet by doing good deeds that are supportive and thoughtful of others.)

SEIZE THE MOMENT

Make eye contact, smile and say something. "Hi!" or "Hello" is the best icebreaker. Maybe the other person is just shy or anxious. Make your conversation so fascinating that other people are drawn into your little group and expand the circle.

> ***When you focus on other people's comfort more than your own, your self-consciousness disappears.***

Remember, the white-knuckled drinker is more uncomfortable than you are, and will welcome your conversation.

4. NAME TAGS THAT PULL

While people still have mixed feelings about name tags, they are very important for business and social events. Name tags have the following obvious benefits:

- You can address a person by name, which is always preferable.
- They provide information you can use to begin conversation (company, job title, location, area of specialty, etc.).
- If you see "that familiar face" but aren't sure if the person is who you think he or she is, you can sneak a peek at the name tag.

At many trade shows, cocktail parties and other events, name tags are provided. The person's name should be large and bold enough in type to be visible even if you are standing a few feet away. The company name is often a bit smaller, and you have to get closer to read it.

Many civic organizations and churches use name tags to encourage mingling. Sometimes the name tags are color-coded to distinguish members from guests or new members. An unwritten rule is that members seek out guests and new members and make them feel welcome.

You might take a cue from this rule, and make yourself an unofficial greeter of guests and new members.

Name "Tag": You're It!

If you are asked to fill out your *own* name tag, you have some leeway in describing your position or specialty. This is a chance to identify yourself in an interesting way. Financial planner Fritz Brauner tells me that when he put the designation "Financial Planner" on his name tag at a business show, no one looked twice. But when he wrote "Money" beneath his name, he was approached by many interesting people who wanted to know what he did.

A sense of humor does help! At a chamber of commerce business social, one member had a name tag that caught my eye and made me laugh. Instead of writing his name, he had written "Name Tag." Corny, but we began a conversation quickly and easily.

If you are planning an event and use computer-generated name tags, be sure the names are big and bold.

Nowadays, technology allows us to "zap" name tags right into our "organizers" and databases. *The Twilight Zone* has arrived, and there is a skill and an etiquette to match this microchip mingling.

PLACEMENT OF YOUR NAME TAG

Always, always place the *name tag on your right-hand side*.
When you extend your right hand for a handshake, the
line of sight is to the other person's right side. If the name
tag is placed on the left side and you sneak a peek away
from the line of sight—you'll get caught! The idea is to
make the name tag as visible as possible.

NO–NAME TAG EVENTS

Name tags are not used at some business and many social
events. (Only in California do you find them even at wed-
dings!) At these events, you're on your own to introduce
yourself to people and engage them in conversation. If
they don't respond, all you can do is move away . . . with
a renewed appreciation for the benefits of name tags.

THE (FORGOTTEN) NAME GAME

We all forget names from time to time, even the names
of people who are important to us. People who must
attend parties, benefits, conventions, fund-raisers and
reunions with humongous numbers of other people can
go into what I call "nomenclature overload"! Name tags
will often prompt that "Bill Smith" that's just on the tip
of your tongue.

We're all inclined to be hard on ourselves if we forget
a name, but as one man said in my El Paso presentation,
"I think we have unrealistic expectations of ourselves. We

meet hundreds of people each week. Our parents may have met only ten new people in a week, and our grandparents perhaps only one! How can we expect to remember all those names?"

If you have forgotten a name or two:

- Say so—with humor.

- *Always* state your own name when greeting another person. (They may have forgotten your name as well.)

- Most people will reply in kind. (Embarrassment of the forgotten name will be averted.)

- Repeat their name. And don't make people struggle to remember your name.

- If you always state your name, you will relieve the other person from "nomenclature overload" and will be remembered kindly.

And if we do forget a name: "Oh, it's been one of those days. I must have run out of RAM" or "So sorry, this is one of those days. I even forgot my own name!"

Never, ever ask, "Do you remember me?" It puts people on the spot and can make for an uncomfortable scene. Mingling mavens don't do that to others.

5. GREAT OPENING LINES

The quest for the perfect opening line may be as old as humankind. Too often we lose an opportunity to meet someone because we spend precious time trying to think of the perfect opening line—and there is no such thing.

The good news is, there are a million perfect openers. What you say will depend upon who you are, the person to whom you are talking, the circumstances, the response you want to get and what pops into your mind. It is far better to say *something* than to wait for the perfect clever remark. Even if what you say isn't going to change the world, don't lose the opportunity to begin a conversation.

Research now supports what expert minglers have always known: The best opening line of all may be a SMILE and a friendly "Hi" or "Hello"!

One opener that's been suggested to me is, "Are you alone by choice or by chance?" That will give you a clue about how to proceed.

Conversation Starters

Common experience is always a good conversation starter. Try talking about:

- the organization or cause
- the venue
- the view
- the food (presentation, calories, taste or lack thereof); beware of whining.
- offering a comment such as "I had a great lunch last week at the convention and visitors bureau event."
- respond with a question like "Oh? Where was it held?"

But what do you actually say? Bring your O.A.R.

OBSERVE

Look around the room. Observe the situation. What is happening? Does there seem to be a good crowd? Do they seem to be enjoying themselves? Was the traffic or the parking difficult? What do these people have in common?

Observations about any of these things might be good conversation starters. Saying something humorous or unexpected is even better.

It's best to avoid negative comments. We don't want to give the impression of being "kvetches" (see Glossary) or whiners. Avoid statements like:

- "The food looks pathetic."
- "This hotel is far more rundown that I had expected."

Go for upbeat, unusual observations that will pique people's interest.

ASK A QUESTION

The questions you ask should be relevant. Do your homework to find out about the group and the people who will be attending the event. Even if you don't know much about the organization, you can ask questions such as the following:

- "What has been the best benefit of joining this group?"

- "How would you suggest I become involved?"
- "How do you know the bride (honoree, groom, 'birthday boy,' anniversary couple, politician, etc.)?"

Questions should be open-ended enough to encourage a response, but not invasive. Here are some sample questions for various events:

Political Fundraiser:

- "What made you decide to support this candidate?"
- "How have you been involved in the campaign?"

Charity Benefit:

- "How did you get involved with the March of Dimes (Leukemia Society, etc.)?"

Professional Association Banquet:

- "Are you a member of this association?"
- "How have you been active in the organization?"

Neighbor's Daughter's Wedding:

- "Do you know the bride or groom?"
- "How did you meet him (or her)?"

Jogging Track:

- "How often do you run here?"
- "How does this compare to the other tracks you've run?"

Qualifying Questions

There are those who advise us to ask a lot of good, smart, open-ended questions and just let the other person talk. WRONG. If all you do is ask questions, and contribute nothing about yourself, your comments or interests, that is *not* conversation. It is an interrogation. There are those of us who are suspicious of the grilling. No matter how charming or interested you may be, conversation is a "duologue."

REVEAL

Disclosing something about yourself is a good way to establish your vulnerability and approachability, but there is a risk involved. Be careful not to reveal anything so personal that it burdens the listener.

Good Openers

- "I don't believe it took me forty-five minutes to get here and I was only three miles away!"
- "It never fails. I always manage to get teriyaki sauce on my tie. At least it highlights the design."
- "This food looks so good, I'm glad I forgot to eat lunch."

Getting to Know You

People do business with people they KNOW, LIKE and TRUST. When we bring who we are (in appropriate amounts) to what we do, we allow others to feel more comfortable and to relate to us.

Self-disclosures should be generally positive. Some time ago, I attended a luncheon meeting for a professional association and said hello to one of the officers. When I asked how he was, he mentioned his separation. Then he elaborated on his teenage children's questions about his love life *and* his sex life. I realized he needed to talk to someone, but that meeting was neither the right time nor the right place . . . and I was not the right person.

The winner of a major bank's Pinnacle Award told me she does not "sell" to her customers. "I just get to know them, their circumstances, and only suggest products that fit their needs and lifestyles. But the key is that I LET THEM GET TO KNOW ME so my calls are always returned, because they are from a *person they know,* not from a banking institution."

Everything in moderation. We want to make sure that we don't burden clients, customers and, even, friends with too much personal information.

Food is almost always a wonderful basis for communication. Grandma knew that food was a great conversation starter . . . that's one reason she made lots of it. It's no accident that meetings, get-togethers, social engagements and family affairs are often centered around a meal. When people come together over food, a certain amount of nurturing takes place—at least on the physical level, and often at the mental and professional levels as well.

"Flirting"—with Disaster

And while we're on the subject of great lines. . . . What about flirting? What about the words, body language, facial expressions and glances that can find their way from a purely social situation to a business setting—or vice versa?

To some, flirting is a way of exchanging friendly banter, very much like small talk. Good-natured, friendly banter is fine, and can be appropriate even in the office.

To others, flirting is a "come-on." It all depends on the flirter, the flirt*ee* and on what is actually being said and done. Flirting is appropriate and even necessary at a singles event. It is a way we signal our interest in others.

Use caution when flirting in a business setting. One person's small talk is another person's come-on. Ask yourself if you want that deal or that promotion, riding on what someone thinks of you as a business associate or as a flirt. No double entendres, no off-color comments, no touching beyond the handshake.

6. MOVING IN: BREAKING AND ENTERING

There is a difference between *including* yourself in other people's conversations and *intruding* on them. Getting into a conversation that is already under way requires a dose of chutzpah, but also some sensitivity. *Watch people's body language and listen to the tone of their conversation for clues.*

One of my clients offers this advice for including without intruding:

- Avoid approaching two people who look as though they are having an intense conversation. If they seem totally preoccupied, you can assume that they are flirting with some profound ideas or with each other.

- Approach groups of three or more who look like they are having fun. Position yourself close to the group. Give only facial feedback to the comments being made. When you feel yourself included, either by verbal acknowledgment or eye contact, you are free to join the conversation. This is *not* the time for you to switch the conversation to you, your product or your agenda. You are the new guest in the group.

- Be open to others who "want in." When you see someone on the periphery of your conversation group, step back. You will have included someone who had been excluded. That is a thoughtful behavior that will make you memorable!

If you merely want to extend a greeting to someone in the conversation, you might say, "Excuse me for interrupting, but I wanted to say hello." Then move away. You may find that your interruption is a welcome relief and that you are invited to stay and chat.

Conversation Interrupters

What if someone interrupts *your* intense or important conversation? According to Dr. Geraldine Alpert, a psychologist in Marin County, north of San Francisco, you can be both firm and gracious. Acknowledge the person politely and thank them for saying hello. Indicate that you need to finish this conversation but will catch up with them later. *Then do so.*

7. MOVING ON: EXTRICATING YOURSELF

Many of us feel uncomfortable with ending a conversation. Someone, somewhere, told us it was rude.

Actually, the etiquette of cocktail parties is that we are *supposed to circulate.* No less an authority than Miss Manners suggests that we spend no more than eight to ten minutes with any one person. We have been invited so that we can mingle and meet the other attendees. It is an opportunity to circulate among peers, colleagues and potential clients, and to meet as many people as possible. The idea is *not* to engage in conversation with one person for the duration, although we sometimes do that because it can be easier. However, in spite of advice to the contrary, we cannot assess business contacts in less than one minute, and conversation with shy people may take much longer.

GRACEFUL EXIT

How to make a graceful exit? I once found myself talking for twenty minutes to someone whose company I didn't find particularly pleasant or stimulating. When the colleague I was with asked why I had done that, I hemmed and hawed and said I hadn't wanted to be rude. "Susan," he said, "why didn't you just say 'EXCUSE ME'?" Now, there's a concept! The following are three ways to leave:

Exit One

To make your exit easier, wait until *you* have just finished a comment. Then smile, extend your hand for a closing handshake and say, "Excuse me, it was nice meeting you." The old "I need to freshen my drink" line has its drawbacks, because theoretically you should ask others if they would like *their* drinks freshened. Then you not only have to return, but you've bought them a drink.

Once you extricate yourself, visibly move one quarter of the room away. It underscores the fact that you really did have someone to see, or something to do, and that you didn't leave that person simply because you were bored. Approach another group or someone else standing alone.

Exit Two

If you spoke to someone who was *not* open nor enjoyable, pleasantly say, I hope you enjoy the rest of the . . . (conference, meeting, party). No need to be rude because he or she may be preoccupied with other worries. Again, move a quarter of the room away.

Exit Three

Take 'em along. Introduce your new pal to other people. You may (or may not) know that when we help people meet others at an event, they remember our kindness. (And we get another "Planet Point.")

Before you leave the event, *be sure to thank the host or hostess.* Even if it is a trade-association luncheon rather than a social dinner party, someone is in charge and has spent time planning the food, the program and all the details of the event. Seek that person out and thank him or her.

Beware of the time-consuming, draining thirty-minute departure, in which you say good-bye over and over again, begin short conversations, say good-bye again, and slowly, painfully inch yourself toward the door. Ronn Owens, a San Francisco radio talk-show host, suggests that when you are ready to leave, LEAVE!

ROANE'S REMINDERS

The following seven strategies will help you work any room.

1. Enter the room with confidence, orient yourself and look for people you either know or *want* to know. And *be nice to everyone!*

2. Go alone or use the Buddy System. Go with a friend or a colleague or a significant other and work the room separately. Most people will not intrude on a conversational pas de deux.

3. Seek out other shy people who will appreciate your interest and conversation.

4. Make the most of name tags. Use the information as a conversation starter, and place the name tag on your right-hand side.

5. Great opening lines come in a million forms. Just about anything will work if it's delivered with a smile and honest interest. Try "Hi!" or "Hello."

6. Don't be afraid to move in and join conversations already in progress, and include those people who want to join your conversation.

7. Moving out of conversations is part of circulating through the room and meeting a variety of new people. Thank the host before you leave.

Advisories:

• Beware of the *Consumption Assumption*. Just because there is an open bar, and we can drink freely, does not mean that we should freely drink! It's still business!

• Treat everyone nicely: You never know!

• Always introduce yourself by your full name to those whose names you can't retrieve.

9

WORKING THE WORDS: SEVEN KEYS TO LIVELY CONVERSATION

You've prepared your presence and worked out your strategies for the event. You're in the room now and mingling with ease. You've even chosen someone you want to meet and introduced yourself with charm . . . and maybe a little chutzpah.

Words are important. The premiere issue of *Talk* magazine noted that "in the telling of history, conversation is overlooked and may pass unrecorded, but it changes the course of history."

SO, WHAT DO YOU SAY NEXT?

Even people who make wonderful self-introductions can be stymied by the next step—*making conversation*.

Initial impressions, be they at events or job interviews, are based on our ability to communicate and converse. The trick is to do so with ease, interest and energy. "Nothing is so contagious as enthusiasm; it moves stones, it charms brutes." This statement is attributed to Edward Bulwer-Lytton in *637 of the Best Things Anybody Ever Said*.

A sincere interest in people is the most important part of being a good conversationalist. If we are just waiting our turn to speak or manipulating others into talking so we can get information, they will know it. We can listen to others not only with our ears, but with our eyes and our whole face to let them know *we care* about their responses, feelings and thoughts.

Be in the moment. Make those two minutes with each person memorable—by giving them your undivided attention. Do not survey the room for the more important, well-known or attractive people.

Your first topic of conversation with a new person probably will *not* be nuclear disarmament, abortion or the possibility of world economic collapse—unless you are at an event organized around these issues.

Probably, you will make small talk. Again, there is nothing small, phony nor unimportant about verbal exchanges that work toward establishing common interests, or allow people to get to know one another better. I'm with Michael Korda: "There is nothing small about small talk."

According to *Brills Content* magazine (March 1999), the number one reason people watch the news is to learn about the weather. Weather is a big topic of interest, and that makes it a good topic to pick because it's what we have in common! It's either raining or snowing or sunny on all of us at the same time.

The following "Seven Keys to Lively Conversation" will help with both the initial small talk and with the more in-depth discussions that may follow. They are designed to make conversation easier and to give you something to say that is interesting and probes for interests you have in common with the other person.

In the workplace, the common threads are obvious, but what builds rapport and relationships and makes the workplace a good setting are the ties and bonds we create with colleagues and coworkers. It's the sense of community that we build by sharing ideas, thoughts, interests and support. Bob Beck, vice president of Scient Corporation, helps their growing staff create "neighborhoods" of special interests so they have a common ground for discussions. "Conversation builds these relationships and ultimately the teams . . . which may be very fluid."

Like everything else, good conversation requires planning! To expand on this topic, I wrote *What Do I Say Next?* because so many people have told me that that is what stymied them the most!

1. READ ONE NEWSPAPER A DAY

Reading a newspaper each day is a must! Even Bill Gates recommended it in a column he wrote several years ago. That is how we glean topics of conversation. Some people balk at this suggestion—until they try it. This is not only the best way I know of to build the "knowledge bank" from which to draw conversation, it can also be fun, entertaining and even addictive! Once you start, it's hard to stop. Whether it is online or on paper . . . the newspaper is full of conversation topics.

"Newstalk" is no substitute for reading the paper.

Television and radio news programs can condense a war into fifteen seconds, a presidential election into thirty seconds. You simply can't get much insight into the issues in that amount of time.

People magazine provides great summary but is also no substitute, and neither are other special interest magazines. Fascinating as these publications may be, they rarely deal in hard news and don't come out daily.

Why should a busy person with a multitude of demands on his or her time read a daily newspaper? *Because a good conversationalist is well-read, well-versed and well-rounded.* He or she knows what is going on in the world, and can talk about it. Reading the paper makes working any room infinitely more manageable.

Information is power. Building that "knowledge bank" lets us contribute to conversations with more ease and interest.

It allows us to be aware of "pop cultcha." One does *not* have to be a "Dead Head" to know about the legacy of Jerry Garcia or a Trekkie to know about Mr. Spock or a teenager to be aware of 98 Degrees or Britney Spears or *Dawson's Creek.*

Do you have to be an expert on everything? Absolutely not. But you must be well-read enough to initiate or contribute to conversations. You need enough knowledge of general topics to pose intelligent questions. *Top Tip:* We must listen to the answers to our questions and comment on them . . . *not* on the price of Nintendos nor Rolls Royces.

Intelligent questions allow others to speak about their own areas of expertise and interest. They also give us the chance to *learn* from what other people say. Every event, meeting or party becomes an educational opportunity that provides us with additional information and resources to "bring to the next banquet."

Vince Deluzio, a partner with a major Pittsburgh law firm, peruses four papers a day. "I go through the Pittsburgh paper, *The Wall Street Journal, The New York Times* and *USA Today.* My job is to be able to make my clients and colleagues comfortable with me." Vince does that. He is a highly regarded member of the community and a mentor to other attorneys.

TIPS FOR PERUSING THE PAPER

- Start with your favorite section first—even if it is the comics. I start with Leah Garchik's column in the *San Francisco Chronicle.* There is usually at least one item that begins my day with a laugh.

- Scan the headlines and first paragraphs if you are pressed for time and won't have a chance to read the whole paper until later. Fortunately, newspapers are written for busy people and so the major elements of any story—the who, what, where, when and how— are almost always covered in the first paragraph.

- Read the business section—whether or not you find it particularly appealing at first. If you have a job or are self-employed, you are in business and you need to know what is going on in the business world. You will be dealing with *other* people who are in business, and you need to know about their concerns.

  The business section isn't nearly as technical or

intimidating as some people suspect. You don't have to be a venture capitalist to understand it. The business of newspapers is to *sell newspapers,* and they can't do this if they don't write things that regular people can comprehend and find interesting.

Reading the business section gives you information that you can use to connect with people. One morning I read that the company for which I was doing a presentation that afternoon had just split its stock. It was important for me to refer to that information both in the presentation and in individual conversations. I was able to tap into something that excited those people and was already a topic of office discussion. Rather than *distracting* them from the stock split with my presentation, I was able to incorporate it and make my talk much more interesting to them.

• Read the sports pages! Even if you aren't an avid fan, you are sure to run into avid fans and this is a tremendous way to build rapport. Our goal in working a room is to make people feel comfortable with us and to create conversation. If other people are interested in the 49'ers or the Cubs or the Maple Leafs, then you are ahead of the game if you know *something* about the sport.

You don't have to memorize batting averages for the last thirty years, but if the World Series is being played in the city where you are doing business, you should at least know what teams are involved and what is happening. It shows that you are well-rounded and that *you care about other people's interests.*

In one of my presentations to CEOs, one CEO said he was at a disadvantage because he did not "follow nor have any interest in sports." He further said, "About ninety percent of my employees, clients, colleagues and associates all talk about sports." What I wanted to say was my brother Ira's favorite refrain for the self-absorbed: "Get over yourself!" But I didn't.

If he already knows that sports is a talk topic of interest to 90 percent of the people in his work life, he is fortunate. It makes conversation easy to start and allows others to be comfortable with your interest. This CEO looked the "gift of gab" horse in the mouth.

- Don't forget the comics. When a particular comic makes me think of someone I know, I often copy and send it or fax it, sometimes with a note. It's a good way to stay in touch, and humor is a wonderful way to connect. My favorite is Hilary Price's "Rhymes with Orange" (and most cartoons in *The New Yorker*).

- Read the lifestyle section. Here you will find features, book excerpts and reviews, humor, commentary, fashion news, and articles on health, social issues and . . . well, lifestyles. The lifestyle section provides a wealth of information for your "knowledge bank," and much of it is perfect for starting and continuing conversations—statistics about stress, careers, divorce, back injuries, diets, commuting, etc.

2. CLIP AND COLLECT

The CSG (Clipping Service Gene) was originally discovered at the University of Illinois, Champaign-Urbana, when I attended college there. Almost every letter from home contained a clipping. "The Relevant Article" was usually a letter to Ann Landers or Dear Abby from a broken-hearted mother whose offspring was at college and (choose one): (a) did not write; (b) did not call . . . unless there was a shortage of funds; (c) did not plan to come home for a holiday; (d) was not lavaliered or pinned; (e) turned down dates with lovely, eligible fellows or gals who were potential candidates for (d) with the future potential of grandchildren

Imagine my dismay when I discovered that CSG, which I identified in *What Do I Say Next?* is an *inherited genetic* trait! The only consolation was that many of my colleagues had also inherited this chromosomal quirk, and it is a great conversation starter.

Clipping and collecting articles and cartoons contributes to conversation—whether these clippings are poignant, satirical, irreverent or informative. Whether they press a hot button or, better yet, a funny bone, our own enthusiasm for whatever piqued our interest can be infectious.

I read about clients, colleagues and business associates in articles from *Fast Company* to the *San Francisco Chronicle* and I always send "an extra copy for the relatives." It is something that I appreciate as well. It is scary when we turn into our parents and do the things that used to drive us nuts! But trust me, it is unavoidable!

3. READ NEWSLETTERS, PROFESSIONAL JOURNALS AND MINUTES

Sometimes we are invited to events sponsored by organizations with which we're not entirely familiar. Such events as charity fund-raisers, political dinners or clients' Christmas parties may require some special preparation. The best way to get a handle on the organization is to read its newsletter or professional journal.

These publications can be invaluable resources. If you invest the time to read them, you will be well compensated. You won't be an "outsider"; you will be familiar with the group and its people, and have all the information you need to ask questions and start conversations.

Should you recognize a member from a photo you saw in the organization's newsletter or journal, you can bet that person will appreciate and welcome you.

The same is true of reading minutes of the organization's meetings. If you are attending a meeting of a new division or group, ask for the minutes of the past three months. You will impress people with your interest, get a better feel for what has been going on in the group and be prepared to contribute interesting and pertinent information to conversations.

Reading a company's newsletter and visiting their website prepares me for events, parties and presentations I am hired to give.

4. TAKE NOTE AND TAKE NOTES

Other people's clever remarks and stories can be interesting, humorous or poignant conversation starters. These statements or situations come from friends, associates, children, people on the street—practically anyone. They happen in the home, the office, at the health club or the hair stylist's—anywhere you have your ears open.

One advantage of these stories is that the hero or heroine is always someone else. Sometimes stories from two different people dovetail. My friend Lana Teplick, a Boston CPA, said of men, "Assume they are all married until proven otherwise." I shared this with another friend, Diane Bennett, and asked her how they might "prove otherwise." She replied, "Ask for their *home* phone numbers."

Lana also provided a terrific tip for parents that I share: "Always be the parent who drives. After a while, the kids think you're part of the steering wheel and continue their conversations as if you're not there. You will always know what is going on!"

Another friend with whom I taught elementary school, Sylvia Cherezian, is mother to two wonderful young men. One day when her son Charles was two, she cried in exasperation, "My God, I've given birth to a child whom I would *never* have allowed in my classroom!" I share that comment with colleagues who mention that they have children and the conversation flows. I don't have children, so remembering these stories allows me to "borrow their lives."

In order to use these comments and situations as conversation starters, we have to *remember* them. Some people write them down in a journal each evening; others carry a small spiral notebook to jot them down or they may use a digital recorder. Even the most unforgettable line or story can get lost if we don't take the time to record it somewhere. To rewrite this book, I had to read and reread a file full of stories I had jotted down. The miracle: that I could read them!

I often share the best piece of advice I received from

my personal mentor, Joyce (Mumsy) Siegel: "Do not spend your time with anyone whom, after you leave, you waste one minute thinking about what they meant by what was said."

People say great things that we can quote . . . that contribute to our conversations.

5. USE HUMOR (SURELY YOU JEST)

Humor has a special way of bringing people together. It can establish rapport and warmth among people. It's a unique and magical elixir that can even heal the body.

Both management and medical research support the value of humor. Laughter is good for your health. "Laughter works by stimulating the brain to produce hormones that help ease pain. It also stimulates the endocrine system, which may relieve symptoms of disease. Laughter can also help feelings of depression," said Dr. William Fry of Stanford Medical School. Since Dr. Fry's original research, we have read volumes about humor as a tonic.

You don't have to be a stand-up comic to use humor. Humor can be defined in two ways. First, it is the quality of being funny, and second, it is the ability to perceive, enjoy or express something that is funny.

The right sentence or phrase at the right moment can save a negotiation or a board meeting. But humor should be used judiciously, because it can offend as well as delight. I'm usually wary when I hear the phrase, "Did you hear the one about the . . . ?" Usually we just read it on a forwarded e-mail!

Humor Dos and Don'ts

- Practice your stories and punch lines. I once practiced my opening story for a presentation seventeen times before the timing was right.

- Watch comedies, both on television and at the movies, and read books about humor. I watch *Will & Grace* with a paper and a pencil by my side (and always attribute the funny lines).

- Use the "AT&T"™ rule to check any story or joke: Is it appropriate? Is it tasteful? Is it timely?

- Laugh at yourself: It is a trait of people who take risks. Some of the best stories are those you tell on yourself.

- Observe for irony. One day I saw a fellow in the lotus position outside Mollie Stone's supermarket. His eyes were closed . . . in a meditative state. And . . . he was smoking a cigarette! Meditative or menthol? Talk about ironic.

- "Don't tell jokes if you don't tell them well," advises Patricis Fripp, internationally acclaimed professional speaker.

- Don't put people down. "Roasting" can create a slow burn—one that can backfire.

- Don't use humor that is racist, sexist, homophobic or "humor" that slurs religion, ethnic origin or disability. (Cantor Rita Glassman shared a version of a nursery rhyme: "Sticks and stones can break my bones and names can only hurt me!")

- Don't be afraid to let go and laugh. It's good for your health and makes working the room a lot more enjoyable.

6. LISTEN ACTIVELY, NOT PASSIVELY

As a raconteur and "talker," I have always been sensitive to the criticism about talkers. But research shows that just because a person is a good "talker" doesn't mean he or she is not also a good "listener."

All of us need to be good listeners, and that means more than staring into someone's eyes while he or she talks—and you plan tomorrow's meeting or rethink the movie you saw last night.

Active listening means *hearing* what people say, concentrating on them and their words and responding. When we really concentrate on that one person and are in the moment, we improve our chances of remembering both the person and the conversation.

In the "How to Work a Room" program, people practice role-playing as "talkers" and "listeners." Thousands of "talkers" have said that the most important behaviors of active listeners, the things that most encouraged them to talk, were what I call The Magnificent Seven:

The Magnificent Seven of Listening

1. Eye contact
2. Nodding
3. Smiling and/or laughing
4. Asking relevant questions that indicate interest
5. Making statements that reflect similar situations
6. Body language that is open and receptive
7. Bringing the conversation full circle

If we are conscious of listening actively, our conversational skills will improve. Working a room will be less work and more fun. Conversation may be a dying art, but with preparation and interest, we can revive it.

7. JUST SAY YES TO NEW OPPORTUNITIES

One way to make interesting conversation is to say yes to opportunities that are out of your realm of expertise or area of interest. I often do that to expand my horizons and "conversation content."

That's why I went rappelling with a friend. It was an exhilarating experience and gave me fuel for conversation! James McCormick is a professional sky diver, and, no, I have not jumped out of an airplane, although several overcrowded, noisy, bumpy flights did make me consider it.

There are some things I do only once; just to know I can and have done them. Like baking bread. Once I made an eggbread (challah) and, to my amazement, it was delicious. I don't have to do that again. There are bakers who make a living baking challah . . . they need my support.

Shayne and Patrick Skov were my companions for an afternoon at Sony's Metreon complex in San Francisco. Seeing it through the eyes of a nine- and seven-year-old was so illuminating. Watching them as they experienced the exhibits, play stations and video games was so much fun. We loved the virtual bowling alley. I still talk about and recommend it to tourists, clients and colleagues who have young children and grandchildren.

When we say yes to new experiences that are out of OUR ordinary realm, we have more to contribute to the conversation of life!

FIVE FUNDAMENTAL LAWS OF CASUAL CONVERSATION

- *Be a conversational chameleon.* Adapt conversation to the individual by age, interest, profession.
- *Be a name dropper.* Always mention the names of people you could have in common.
- *Borrow other people's lives.* Share the stories of your friends who have kids, websites, who study tai kwon do, are Xtreme athletes, have opera tickets—even if you don't.
- *Be a two-timer.* Give people a second chance.

- *Be nice to everyone.* Don't judge tomorrow's book by today's cover.

FIVE FATAL FLAWS OF CASUAL CONVERSATION

- being unprepared
- not reading papers, trade journals, information sources
- controlling conversations by asking a barrage of questions, no matter how open-ended
- complaining (kvetching); telling a series of jokes
- one-upping/competing; interrupting; not listening; putting down others

ECHOING THE SOUNDS OF SILENCE

Silence has its place in conversation. As the late Professor Morrie Schwartz of Brandeis University, in *Tuesdays with Morrie,* asked rhetorically: "What is it about silence that makes us so uncomfortable?" It allows us to consider what we have heard.

When we are asked to speak to an audience, conversing with them before our presentation is engaging and easier when we employ the Seven Keys.

ROANE'S REMINDERS

Remeber the Seven Keys to Lively Conversation:

1. Read one local newspaper a day and a national paper online or on paper. Location, national, international conversation starters fill the pages.

2. Clip and collect cartoons, announcements or articles of interest to you and your network. Send them!

3. Read newsletters, professional journals and minutes for up-to-the-minute topics of conversation.

4. Take note and take notes when you hear something interesting or observe the odd or absurd.

5. Use humor (surely you jest) carefully. Be light-hearted and don't take yourself so seriously. No "dissing" of others.

6. Listen actively—with ears, eyes and heart. Truly pay attention.

7. Just say yes to new opportunities. Doing, seeing, visiting something new and out of our everyday interests . . . gives us something to talk about.

10

HOW TO WORK
AN AUDIENCE

You've been invited to give a presentation to your local chamber of commerce, Rotary Club, college alumni, professional association or local high school career day. You get a queasy feeling in your stomach and dry mouth!

It has been said that the number one fear is public speaking. Not true. The most uncomfortable situation that creates fear is walking into a room full of strangers, which most people have to do. But public speaking is also daunting and ranks as our number two fear.

Giving a speech to strangers! Talk about a double-whammy stomach churner. Remember, if you were invited to speak to a group, it is due to your knowledge, experience, success. People think you have something to contribute. Congratulations! That is a huge compliment.

One of the most effective skills we can develop is our ability to speak in front of an audience. CEOs do it all the time. When I was a teacher, it was a skill that I taught my students. It was *not* easy to get the shy kids to take this "risk." But I knew they would have to present team projects in high school and that their oral presentation skills would serve them well in their futures. It was my job as their teacher to prepare them.

As you can imagine, I was *not* the most popular teacher. Because I also taught grammar, punctuation and research skills, my rep as the tough teacher of the boring subjects was already sealed.

Truth be told, I also made the students listen and behave. It was *not* enough for my students to write a grand paper or deliver it as an oral presentation. The students had to have good audience behavior for the other students' presentations, as they were graded on that, too.

How can *we* ensure good audience behavior? Simple, *"work" the audience ahead of time!* As a professional speaker who has spoken to hundreds of audiences ranging from thirty to three thousand, I have been my own warm-up act. When we warm up the audience, they are receptive to us and our presentation. In a nutshell, TALK to audience members BEFORE you are introduced to speak.

REMEDIES FOR THE ROADBLOCKS

These are not strangers. You have something in common with them. Maybe it's your profession, your community, your membership in a nonprofit organization or members of your board of directors. Or maybe it's a sales presentation to potential clients.

Introduce yourself. Look at their name tags. Make a

comment, observation or ask a question about the information.

- "Nice to see you." (with a firm handshake, eye contact and a smile)
- "What brings you to the event?"
- "Oh, I'm originally from Chicago. Where did you go to high school?"
- "Great tie. I see you're a *South Park* fan, too. Cartman is my favorite character."

GREETING AND MEETING

You can be the "greeter" at the door as attendees enter the room, which I have done. People were so surprised and pleased to be "welcomed" into the conference luncheon, let alone by their speaker. Or walk into the audience as they are being seated and greet them. Move around the room. You don't have to talk to each person, but do make sure you are in each section. Do include others by initiating eye contact. Get to the back of the room because the people who go for the seats in the last few rows may need the most "warming up."

The people with whom you have chatted will pay attention because you're now a person, not just a presenter. There is now a personal connection. The audience members who saw you talk to others get that same sense.

You have engaged your audience. They are now ready to listen to you. You have set the tone.

SPEAKING OF (PUBLIC) SPEAKING

Corporate speech coach and first female president of the National Speakers Association Patricia Fripp says, "There is no such thing as private speaking. Whether it is at a presentation, an investors' meeting, or a trade show, it's public, unless you are alone, talking to yourself."

TIPS FOR TERRIFIC TALKS

- *Know* your audience. Ask the program chairperson several questions:

  - Who will attend?
  - How many will attend?
  - What is the audience demographic?
  - How is the program billed?
  - What is the goal for your program?
  - Who else is on the program and/or your panel?
  - What are the needs of the group?
  - Why were you invited?

- *Read* the group's newsletter, trade journals, program brochure.
- *Visit* their website.
- *Interview* several people who will attend.
- *Prepare* your material. Get comfortable using the visuals, if you plan to do so.

- *Practice* so you are familiar with the three key points, subpoints and vignettes that support your points.
- *Attend* their receptions.
- *Greet and meet* members of the audience.

You have just had conversations with audience members. Continue that conversation from the platform when you deliver your presentation. Talk *with* the audience, not at them.

OPENING LINES

Unless you are a great joke teller and writer, DON'T start with a joke, unless you wrote it. Many people will have heard it or read it on e-mail. Start with a story/vignette that happened to you or someone you observed or that you were told in conversation or overheard. DO NOT tell a story that you heard often or that another speaker has used. It is his/her material, not yours. You run the risk of retelling a vignette the audience already knows. Boring.

Tell YOUR own vignettes. The "stories" are everywhere. OBSERVE. LISTEN. Write them immediately. Start telling these fun, ironic, odd occurrences to your friends. Observe their reactions. Brainstorm with yourself. Go to your favorite thinking place with a Mead spiral index card book (any drugstore has them). Write one vignette per index card.

I take my aerobic walks with Post-it™ notes and pads of paper in my fanny pack. Sometimes I have to stop during my walk to write. If I don't the thought disappears. Once I was aerobic walking, talking to myself and voilà! the title of a chapter popped into my brain . . . and the concept (How to Work the Techno-Toy Room). Because I keep paper and pen in my fanny pack, I wrote it down immediately or I would have lost the thought.

Be ready for ideas at all times. Have a microcassette or digital recorder or pads of paper everywhere!

Gather your own material and your presentation will be unique and yours alone. Include research stats and comments from the experts; attribute all sources (otherwise it is plagiarizing). This shows you did your homework.

Treat your audiences as the intelligent people they are. You may know a lot about Java Script, web design, financial planning, a new surgical procedure or stress management, but don't act patronizing.

Customize your program for the needs and the members of the audience. I was on a program with General Colin Powell, who took the time to do his homework and made his presentation relate to his audience of restaurant managers. So should we all! And I took notes, learned and was smitten with General Powell's down-to-earthiness.

If the thought of a presentation to clients, potential clients, colleagues or community is so uncomfortable, join a Toastmasters group. Or start one in your company. The rewards will be well worth the time you invest.

And if you "work" your audience before you speak, you will be a hit!

SOME ADDITIONAL THOUGHTS

Listen to other speakers. The people who do it most often are standing at the pulpits in churches, temples and synagogues. Attend company programs where your CEO is speaking. If you are the CEO, attend the conference board sessions or industry conferences.

Listen to tapes of the great orators. Go to comedy clubs and observe the stand-up comics. Take a class in comedy or improvisation. Attend your local National Speakers Association's meetings.

At the CEO/executive level, work with a speech coach. I do and have worked with executive speech coach Dawne Bernhardt for over sixteen years. Her manner of giving feedback is so gracious that she is a role model as well.

Go to live performances and observe how entertainers "work" their audiences. Dame Edna (comedian Barry Humphries) is masterful. The Divine Miss M (Bette Midler) taught me a technique I now use. And Bill Cosby's use of the handheld microphone to create voices and sounds is instructive. But please note, as a presenter you do not have license to "pick on" any audience members as the entertainers may do.

If you talk with your audience, you will never need a gimmick or have to do "shtick" to capture their attention.

ROANE'S REMINDERS

- Hone your public-speaking skills.
- "Work" your audience by greeting, meeting and conversing with them prior to your program.
- Introduce yourself. Use name tags for conversation; move into and around each section of the audience.
- Prepare for your presentation.
- Start with an attention-getting observation, vignette or statistic.
- Collect the "stories" daily. Fun, interesting, odd and ironic occurrences happen all the time.
- Customize your presentation for the audience.
- Listen to other speakers and the great orators.
- Observe entertainers to see how they engage the audience.
- Practice your presentation so that it flows like a conversation.
- Join Toastmasters.
- Work with an experienced, qualified speech coach.

11

WORKING THE RULES OF ETIQUETTE: GOOD MANNERS EQUALS GOOD BUSINESS

Mention the words "etiquette" or "good manners" and the most boring or vacuous conversation or meeting becomes highly charged. Why would such old-fashioned terms create that lively interest? One reason is that manners and etiquette seem to be disappearing. I wrote that twelve years ago and the situation has deteriorated over the past decade.

Many people are too "busy" or preoccupied with "more important things" to practice common courtesies—responding to R.S.V.P.s, extending a "thank you," making good introductions and treating others with courtesy and respect. Some people, it seems, were never taught the "niceties"—thoughtfulness and consideration. Yet bad manners can be deadly . . . both to the reputation and to the bottom line. It's not nice to hurt people's feelings or offend sensibilities, and it's not good business practice, either.

The opposite is true as well. "If you have a great product, a commitment to service, and treat your customers and employees with common courtesy, the market share will take care of itself," says Tom Peters, guru, author and speaker.

How are we *supposed* to behave at a party, reception or convention? In general? The answer: VERY WELL!

But what is "behaving well"? The expectations are much the same as those that parents and teachers have of children:

1. Know the rules.
2. Observe the rules.
3. Do so graciously.

If you don't already know the rules of formal etiquette and business etiquette, it's wise to learn them. Many good references are available in bookstores and libraries.

The problem is, so many of the rules have changed that even people who were taught in various "white-glove" schools of etiquette often don't have any idea what they're doing. Experts are scrambling to write books on "new etiquette," "business etiquette," "sexual etiquette," "teen etiquette," "interNETiquette"—you name it! Clearly, things have changed.

ETIQUETTE AND MANNERS

Etiquette is defined as "the usages and rules for behavior in polite society, official or professional life." Certain basic rules are still accepted as the norm, and it behooves us to know both the *old* etiquette and the *new* etiquette. The executive suites of corporate America require it.

But knowing the rules of etiquette is not enough. What we're really after is manners—that wonderful combination of courtesy, caring and common sense.

There is a difference between knowing the rules of etiquette, being a person of manners and the manner in which we relate to others. Some people follow every rule of etiquette but have a manner that is rude or patronizing.

There is an old story about a Washington hostess who noticed that one of her guests used the wrong fork at a formal dinner and pointed out this error to him in front of the other guests. She knew the proper etiquette, but showed a lack of good manners. Why? *People with good manners don't embarrass others.*

In contrast, when Lady Astor's guest picked up the wrong fork, she picked up the wrong fork, too, so that he wouldn't be embarrassed.

Noah Griffin, San Francisco PR specialist, says that "people with manners are those who treat others in such a way that everyone is comfortable with them." He has noticed that the younger members of an exclusive San Francisco men's club seem unaware of gracious behavior.

People with good manners also treat others with respect. Knowing the rules is one thing; caring about people and treating them with consideration is something else.

Bob Beck is vice president of Scient Corporation. He has often been asked whom he credited with giving him the most help in his career. People want to learn the name of this important mentor. "My mother," Bob said. "She not only taught me that I could do whatever I tried, but also how to treat people *courteously*." Bob is now one of the experienced guys at a fast-growing company of young people who are lucky enough to learn from this special person.

Courtesy is the cornerstone of good manners. According to my *Standard Collegiate Dictionary,* "to be courteous is to be polite while having a warmer regard for the feelings and dignity of others."

This is reflected in our use of the techno toys, phones, radios and even the stereo! It's how we behave with clients, coworkers, friends, family and strangers.

If people are comfortable with us, our presence at any event will be valued. And we will be remembered . . . for the right reasons.

John Rosemond, a psychologist and syndicated columnist, recently wrote that manners and character are inseparable. He quoted the esteemed Rebbe (Rabbi Menachim Mendel Schneerson), who extolled the virtue of a solid foundation of character. Manners matter and say volumes about us and our character.

MANNERS MAVENS

The bad news is that the rules have changed . . . and continue to change, and at warp speed.

The good news is that it's easy to get help. The changing rules of etiquette have spawned a whole new industry. Books, columns, seminars and even software programs and websites on etiquette are readily available. There is a great demand for expert consultants who can show us the acceptable conventions for social and business behavior, because people *want to know.* That is one of the reasons my presentations have been so popular in the business world. People need the reminders.

Miss Manners (to whom you may write only in blue or blue-black ink—never peacock blue) has written several books and has a syndicated column. Letitia Baldrige (or Miss Manners), former social secretary to Jackie Kennedy, has written both *Letitia Baldrige's Complete Guide to Executive Manners* and a revised edition of *Amy Vanderbilt's Complete Book of Etiquette.* There is a plethora of practical guides.

Baldrige claims that manners are 99 percent common sense and 1 percent kindness.

THE R.S.V.P.

R.S.V.P. stands for *"Répondez s'il vous plait."* This translates from the French as "Respond if you please." (And if you don't, you may not get invited again—at least to my house.)

A social invitation requires a response. That's all there is to it. To compensate for a general deterioration in etiquette, response cards are often included in invitations. These days, people have added phone numbers and e-mail addresses, just so they can figure out the guest tally and how much food to order. (Notice I didn't say "prepare"!)

R.S.V.P. FOR BUSINESS

R.S.V.P.s for business events, meetings and association luncheons are a bit different. The expectation is that you will preregister and prepay or will call in a reservation. And you are expected to attend if you reserve! You generally do not have to call to say you won't be able to attend unless you've already responded and committed to being there.

It's not good manners or good business to be a "drop-in." I have attended many luncheons where too many "busy" people (*much* too busy to bother calling in a reservation) showed up at the door at the last minute. The food count was thrown way off balance—and so was the luncheon's chairperson! Leftovers for an army (or worse, a shortage of shrimp puffs) is every host's nightmare.

If you find out at the last minute that you'll be able to attend after all, at least call the morning of the event to let them know you're coming.

Several clients told me horror stories of commitment-phobics who never R.S.V.P. lest they have to show up. One woman told me that at least fifteen people sent in R.S.V.P.s for her wedding and did *not* show. The cost was about $1,250 . . . and several friendships!

To R.S.V.P. shows good manners, good business, consideration, breeding and respect.

RSVP@MINDYOURMANNERS.COM

The Internet has added another spin on the dial. There are now several online invitation sites that "allow recipients to see the invitation list and can use the information to decide whether to RSVP," according to Carrie Kirby in the *San Francisco Chronicle* (January 20, 2000). Oy vey! (See Glossary.)

Fast, expedient and oh so, impersonal. While the online invite and R.S.V.P. sites may work for a big bash, I hope they do not supplant the wedding, christening, bar mitzvah and baby shower invitations that arrive with a stamp . . . and my stamp of approval. Just because things are easier doesn't make them correct.

INTRODUCTIONS

Many people feel awkward about introductions because they remember being taught that there was one right way to do it—and they can't remember what that one right way is. So they stand there, with two people whom they want to introduce, stammering, "Uh . . . Jon, meet Susan . . . uh, no . . . Susan, Jon. My friend . . . uh . . ." Much of the warmth goes out of an introduction when we don't feel comfortable.

It helps if there is a reception line. If you see one, head directly for it and introduce yourself to the host. Give some information about yourself that he or she can pass on as you are introduced to the next person in line. If there is no reception line, take a deep breath and rely on the strategies we've discussed. If you spot people with "host" badges, introduce yourself to them and hope that they will introduce you around.

Letitia Baldrige makes introductions very simple in her book *The Complete Guide to Executive Manners*. She says that the most important thing to remember about introducing people is *to do it*, "even if you forget names, get confused or blank out on the proper procedure."

Ms. Baldrige's Guidelines for Introductions

"Introducing people is one of the most important acts in business life . . ."

1. Introduce a younger person *to* an older person.
2. Introduce a peer in your own company *to* a peer in another company.
3. Introduce a nonofficial *to* an official person.
4. Introduce a junior executive *to* a senior executive.
5. Introduce a fellow executive *to* a customer or client.

The idea is always to introduce the "less important" person to the "more important" person. (We know these people aren't really less or more important on a human level, but we're dealing here with arbitrary societal conventions.) What if the CEO is younger than the person you want to introduce? Use common sense and assess the situations on a case-by-case basis.

Some examples:

"Mr. Cummins, I'd like to present my daughter Cynthia. Cynthia, this is Mr. Sherwood Cummins, the president of our company."

"Mr. and Mrs. Henricks, I'd like to introduce to you a fellow executive from Standard Oil, Timothy Anderson. Tim, this is Mr. and Mrs. Scott Henricks, good friends of my parents."

About using people's titles she says, "When introducing people of equal standing, you do not have to use a title unless you are introducing an older person, a professional or someone with official rank." In other words, you might use the "titles" of Dr. Glasser, Senator Boxer, Father Paul or Rabbi Weiner—but the two new vice presidents might be simply Jennifer Walker and Michael Berringer.

When introducing a public official, use his or her title even if he or she no longer holds the position. You would say either "Mayor Koch" or "former Mayor Koch," "President Carter" or "former President Carter."

Proper etiquette is important in introductions, but we shouldn't become such slaves to it that we lose our warmth or our humor. The most important thing is that people know you *want* them to meet one another. When in doubt, just give the names and some indication of who the people are and what they might have in common. And say so with respect and regard and enthusiasm.

Never "shorten" someone's formal name unless they invite you to do so. My name is Susan, not Sue. I know Roberts, Davids, James and Judiths who do *not* go by Bob, Dave, Jim or Judy.

NAMING NAMES

People like to be remembered . . . *by name.* But it's not easy to remember everyone, particularly if we meet a lot of people.

The classic Name Nightmare. . . . You are at a reception for a local charity, attended by about two hundred

people and held in the ballroom of a local hotel. A man
approaches you and says, "Craig, it's so good to see you
again!"

Your mind races, your heart pounds, a bead of perspi-
ration forms on your brow. You don't have a clue who
this person is.

What to do? Pretend you don't see or hear him, turn
and make a hundred-yard dash across the room? Duck
under the buffet table? Beat your breast and throw yourself on his mercy?

Obviously not. The best solution is to tell the truth . . .
preferably with some humor. You might try:

"Forgive me. It's been such a busy day, I barely
remember my own name."
"Please, help me out. I've just gone blank . . . it's
genetic."

Who is going to say, "No, I want to watch you
squirm until you remember my name"?

By the same token, don't let people squirm to remember *your* name or who you are. Always state your name
clearly, immediately and with energy. Give the other person some idea of who you are or how you may have met.

Memory expert Dr. Joan Minninger, author of *Total
Recall* (a memory book), offers some tips for remembering
names. The first is to *decide to remember.* She recommends that we say our name, and repeat the other person's name, while shaking hands—because this physical
gesture makes for kinesthetic reinforcement. Looking for
an unusual physical characteristic and focusing on it also
helps connect the name with the face.

And, finally, for those of us who did not grow up in California (where everyone is called by his or her first name), there is the problem of what to *call* people. Do we use the first name, the Mr., Mrs. or Ms. form or the formal title?

Option #1: Use the formal title (Dr. Baumann, Ms. Elkins, General Powell, Supervisor Gonzalez). People who want you to call them by their first names will invite you to do so. "Please call me Jim." If they don't offer the first name, stick to the title.

Option #2: Ask. "Do you prefer to be called Dr. Glasser?"

THANK-YOUS

Not everyone writes thank-you notes these days, but it is an extremely gracious gesture and one that is appreciated by every host or hostess. Think of how you would feel if you'd had ten people to dinner. Wouldn't it be nice to get a note from someone thanking you for all you'd done to make the evening pleasant?

A former professor and educational consultant said, "If I take the time to plan the menu, shop, clean the house, cook, serve the dinner and clean up, that may take four to six hours! My guest certainly has a few moments to write a note or card to say thank you."

With the desire to be memorable and stand out from the crowd so prevalent, sending thank-you notes makes a lasting, positive impression.

To write or to word-process? Handwritten notes are quickly becoming a lost art, and some people complain that it takes too much time to write thank-you notes by hand. But most "manners mavens" agree that the hand-written note is more valued. It reflects personal care, thought and time expended. An e-mail can be sent as a quick acknowledgment, followed by the handwritten note or card.

When we take the time to personalize our notes we distinguish ourselves from the crowd and become memorable.

A grandmother of my acquaintance told me how she "taught" her college student granddaughter the importance of a thank-you note. "Two Christmases ago I sent Wendy a check as is my habit. *Not* a word! Last year, I sent *nothing*. Wendy called and told me she had not received her usual check for Christmas. 'Really, when I did not receive your thank-you for my Christmas gift, I assumed you did not want or need my money.' Wendy apologized profusely. But I sent nothing. That year she was more attentive to her old grandma. When this year's Christmas gift arrived, she called immediately *and* sent an exquisite note."

Reprinted with special permission of King Features Syndicate.

MISCELLANEOUS MANNERS (THREE TIPS)

1. People expect that we will "bring something to the banquet." That means, at the very least, energy, enthusiasm, conversation, information and humor. Approach people with a smile, a handshake and an open, upbeat greeting. And look them in the eye. Invite people into your conversations once they get started.

2. Don't let your good time go up in smoke. Smoking is a burning issue. We may have the legal right to smoke in some places, but it is offensive to many people and may not be prudent.

3. Judging people by their appearances can be a grievous error.

It's important to consult the "manners mavens" to keep abreast of changing patterns in etiquette, but it's even more important to be a person of manners—one who genuinely cares about other people and makes an effort to make them feel comfortable. Manners are a combination of common sense and kindness.

Do the gracious thing, the thing you would like done if you were in the other person's place—whether you are responding to invitations, making introductions or extending a "thank-you."

The bottom line: Be nice, and be thoughtful and considerate of others, even in the techno-toy room.

ROANE'S REMINDERS

- Good manners equals good business.

- We are never too busy to bypass common courtesy—which is having a regard for the feelings and dignity of others.

- Don't save nanoseconds. Invest time in the "niceties."

- Know the Rules of Etiquette:

  - table manners
  - introductions
  - guest and host behavior
  - cyberspace

- R.S.V.P. . . . don't show up without having done it, forget to attend or wait for better offers.

- Don't presume informality: Wait until it is offered.

- Thank-you *notes* are a sign of acknowledgement, appreciation and manners.

- Send thank-yous for the tangibles—gifts, checks, meals—and the intangibles—ideas, leads, referrals, advice and listening.

- Never shorten someone's name unless told to do so. ("Please call me Dave" is the invitation to do so.)

GO!

12

WORKING THE COCKTAIL PARTY WITH PLEASURE, PURPOSE AND PANACHE

You're all set. You've reviewed the roadblocks and applied the remedies. You've focused on the potential benefits and prepared both your presence and your strategies. You are ready to converse with just the right balance of chutzpah and charm, and you know your manners as well as your etiquette.

Now it's time to take that wealth of knowledge and that enthusiasm for mingling out into the world. In the next few chapters, we will focus on five of the "rooms" that are now at your feet: the cocktail party, the reunion, the techno-toy room, the trade show and . . . yes, the world!

The cocktail party is here to stay as a business and a social function. Surviving them is good; making the most of them and having a good time in the process is even better!

Cocktail parties are gatherings of about two hours where drinks and finger food are served and guests are expected to stand and to circulate. There are three basic types of cocktail parties:

- social,
- business,
- fund-raiser (charitable, civic, political, etc.).

People have wanted detailed "mingling maps" and have mentioned C. Northcote Parkinson's "Laws of Moving Through the Cocktail Party." I recently learned that his writing on the subject were *satirical* in intent. When you are prepared, observe the room and feel confident no map is needed. Just your good manners, conversation and interest in others, whether they are standing near a wall or the dessert table.

THE SOCIAL COCKTAIL PARTY

The social cocktail party is making a comeback. It never really disappeared, but it is more popular now than ever because it is a simpler process than a sit-down dinner and can more easily be used to reciprocate social obligations. You can return invitations without hiring a staff of twenty or spending a week making food. Calling a caterer is my preference.

Heavy sit-down dinners are also less common because we have become a nation of "grazers." We want a sliver of this and a taste of that. We love to nibble and nosh (see Glossary), to experiment and combine different kinds of foods.

The social cocktail party may have a theme or be an "occasion" party based on holidays or other specific events. It might celebrate an engagement, a housewarming, Halloween, Valentine's Day or simply be that the host/hostess felt like having a party and inviting his or her friends to meet one another. I hosted a cocktail party at a local restaurant for my friends and colleagues. The theme: a tenth birthday party for my "baby," *How to Work a Room*. I even had napkins to match and did not have to cook or clean!

If there is a written invitation, you will probably be asked to R.S.V.P. and you must definitely do so. For my party—which required a "head count" for the restaurant, I called three people who had not called in to R.S.V.P. Will they be invited to my next soiree? Who knows? If your hosts request specific attire (costumes, casual, black-tie optional, etc.), adhere to it. It is their party, and they have put some effort into planning it. Don't let them be the only ones in the room wearing gorilla suits or black tie.

Unless someone buttonholes you immediately after you walk in the door, your first stop will be the hosts. It is their job to meet, greet and introduce you to others. Good hosts always have a vignette or two about each guest that makes introductions easier and more interesting.

After you have begun to meet people, remember that parties are for *mingling* and *circulating*. The hosts have invited you so that you can meet their other friends. It's rude to latch on to one person and sit in the corner with that person for the rest of the evening.

A tip to hosts: Placing the food and beverages at different locations around the room encourages guests to circulate.

At the social cocktail party, you can always fall back on "How do you know Arlynn (the host)?" for a conversation starter.

Even though the party may be purely social, you, of course, never leave home without your business cards and so you will have a good supply of them with you. You might meet your biggest client of the year, your new best friend or someone who can coach your daughter's soccer team.

Even if the encounter is completely social—or perhaps even romantic—business cards are a better and safer way to exchange information than scrawling phone numbers on wine-soaked napkins with filthy old golf pencils or thrashing around in your purse or wallet for deposit slips. Is this the way you want the relationship to begin?

And remember: Thank the hosts before you leave.

THE BUSINESS COCKTAIL PARTY

Business cocktail parties come in several varieties:

1. the no-host reception before the professional association meeting,
2. the office party, which may celebrate anything from the company's IPO to an anniversary or a holiday,
3. the business social, which is often sponsored by the chamber of commerce, the convention and visitors bureau or some other civic organization.

THE NO-HOST COCKTAIL RECEPTION

The no-host reception is usually forty-five minutes to an hour long and precedes a business luncheon or a dinner meeting. You register for the reception when you register for the meeting, and there is generally a no-host bar.

This is a time for members to reconnect with one another, and to meet new people who have been brought as guests. It is also an opportunity for you to bring guests who might be interested in joining the association. If you are a guest, it is a time for you to find out about the organization. For both members and guests, it is a great opportunity to interact.

There is usually no official host at these events, but there is often a greeting committee. Introduce yourself to someone on the committee. They should find at least one other person to whom they can introduce you, and then you're on your own. Pull out your bag of tricks, warm up your smile and begin to work the room!

Conversation starters are everywhere at these events. If you are a guest, you can ask questions about the organization and the various ways of participating. If you are already a member, this is a time to renew acquaintances and meet new people in your field. You will also want to extend yourself to guests and new members so that they feel more comfortable and welcome.

THE BONNIE RAITT/SUSAN ROANE METHOD OF MINGLING

Let's give them "something to talk about." I always wear a pin: a star, a telephone, a frog. . . . This opens conversations. Secretary of State Madeleine Albright also wears "brooches," and her circle "broaches" difficult peace talks. But she provides the conversation piece.

Men have worn ties that give us "something to talk about." Looney Toons, Mickey Mouse, Jerry Garcia, *South Park,* and holiday ties open up conversations. I found a great Three Stooges tie for my brother Michael, the lawyer—Moe, Curly and Larry faces with the names Dewey, Cheatem and Howe, attorneys at law. He told me the "boys" are quite the conversation starter. Nyuk! Nyuk!

Remember, these gifts of gab must be "opened"! When you see a unique lapel pin, brooch or tie—say something! You are being invited to say hello!

> *Being approachable is just as important as approaching others; and a smile and eye contact are essential.*

Remember—the focus here is BUSINESS, with a social flair, to be sure, but it's still important to do your homework and work the room so that you make new contacts and strengthen old ones.

This kind of cocktail reception is usually followed by a sit-down meal, a program and announcements. So even when the reception is over, you have another opportunity to meet people during the meal.

THE MEAL: SIT DOWN, YOU'RE ROCKING THE BOAT!

The first rule: Do *not* sit with people you know. If you just wanted to spend time with your friends, you could have gone out for a pizza. This is a chance to meet seven to nine new people, all of whom have something in common with you. Don't miss the opportunity!

Be the table host. Introduce yourself to the group at the table and ask the others to do the same. This is a risk, but the rewards are great. The person you really want to talk to could be sitting on the other side of the table, rather than next to you. If you hadn't gone around the table and introduced yourselves, you might never have known that he was there. After the meal is over, there will be time for a more private conversation, and you will have him pinpointed.

The dress for these occasions is usually what you would wear to the office, but it can get a bit tricky around the holidays. Several years ago I attended the holiday party of a local professional association. I was wearing a dressy suit; one of the other women wore a strapless long gown. One of us was dressed inappropriately. I never figured out which one. When in doubt, make some subtle inquiries.

THE OFFICE PARTY

The office or company party is a different kind of animal from the no-host reception before a professional association meeting. *It is business,* despite the trappings that may confuse us—music, formal invitations, dancing, drinking, etc.

If clients are in attendance, you are also a host— whether or not you own the company or firm. One year I was asked to give a presentation to members of a law firm because they had hosted a party for clients and potential clients. And the attorneys had talked to each other! A costly waste of time and money. *Act like a host* and your guests will be welcomed.

Remember the cautions about alcohol consumption, appropriateness of conversation and humor, and the need for business greeting etiquette even if your coworkers have forgotten them and are running around the typing pool with lampshades on their heads. That's no way to work a room.

One of the most fun parties was thrown by my buddy Guy Kawasaki for a celebration of garage.com. Guy, author of *Rules for Revolutionaries,* was featured in the *San Jose Mercury News* as the man who "works" Silicon Valley . . . to which, I would add, "like a mensch" (see Glossary). He was the most congenial host, spending time with each guest, the garage.com staff and the venture-capital gang. He made sure we all had T-shirts, books, lots of food and fun!

The office Christmas/holiday party is notorious for bad behavior. I've heard many stories of inebriation, sickness, flirtations and dalliances that have caused people to lose promotions and, sometimes, jobs. Even the office holiday party is business. Go to have a good time in the spirit of the holiday season, but don't exceed the bounds of taste or reason. But do attend.

Dancing and relaxing are definitely *not* out of line. But leave the "dirty dancing" for a nonbusiness occasion. (If the event is a dinner-dance, you may want to take a few dance lessons if you are not comfortable on the dance floor.) This is a good chance to chat with colleagues in a less pressured setting. It may also be a great time to give kudos to those who have helped you, or who have been particularly encouraging or supportive.

Spousal Support

Spouses who attend office parties should be treated as individuals in their own right and not just as appendages of the person who works with you. It's not easy being a spouse at an office party, and the person who makes an effort to meet and chat with spouses is always appreciated. Try to find out what the spouse's interests are instead of talking only about your colleague and the work you share.

Remember, most spouses today work, are involved in the community and have interests that may match your own. Be mindful of how you talk to your own spouse. No one wants to listen to put-downs, digs and comments reflective of "Family Feud." Sadly, I have observed this behavior firsthand and it was very disconcerting.

THE BUSINESS SOCIAL

The business social is often called the "After Hours" and it has become a staple of many convention and visitors bureaus, chambers of commerce and other civic organizations. It is an event made to order for creating visibility and meeting other businesspeople in your city.

These functions are usually held about once a month and are open to members and their guests. People who attend them have in common:

- membership in the organization,
- business interest in the community.

That represents a wide range of conversation starters!

Research shows that it is easier to remember a person's profession than it is to remember his or her name. At the business social, people usually talk about what they *do*.

This is no accident. The business social is one of the best forms of free advertising anywhere—if you know how to work the room. I faithfully attended my San Francisco convention and visitors bureau business socials, and actually do much of my "hands-on" research at these events across the nation. I've met people at these events who have become dear friends as well as valued associates. I've gained more visibility than I could possibly have afforded through advertising, and great material for my books and talks. I've described "working a room" as what you do if no one left you an inheritance for the advertising budget.

The business social is not usually a place to finalize deals or sign contracts; it's a place to meet people, get to know them better and discover what you have in common and how you might support one another—even if it is "only" moral support. In spite of what some sales experts claim, it's an opportunity to establish rapport, not to close a sale.

People do business with people they know, like and trust. Again, etiquette, manners and courtesy are the keys.

No matter how clear your focus, the impression you create depends on your ability to communicate a genuine caring, a sincere generosity of spirit and likability.

A caveat: We cannot *know* people in the first sixty seconds! We know our reactions to their voice, comments, clothes, style. But we do not know of their good hearts, charitable ways, family connections or network. Or their evil ways, disrepect for coworkers or the law. There is no such thing as the "One-Minute Mingler."

THE FUND-RAISER: YOUR MONEY OR . . .

The third type of cocktail party is the fund-raiser. Its purpose is to benefit a charity or community organization. Or it may be to "honor" a politician or political hopeful by raising funds for the campaign coffers.

Carl La Mell, as the CEO/president of Clearbrook, must attend many of these events. Due in large part to his style of fund-raising and gathering support, he took his former association (Victor Neumann) and expanded it from a base of $500,000 to a base of $10.5 million. He says, "After working a full day, I rarely *want* to go to a cocktail party or reception. But once I am there, I am ready to do my job *and* have a good time."

When *we* are having a good time, our enthusiasm generates enthusiasm in others. They want to be around us, and to do business with us.

La Mell's Latest Advice for Working Fund-raisers

1. Know who you have to see.
2. Make sure they *do not* know that it's your goal to see them.
3. Do not talk about business. Make the connection, set rapport and make sure they know who you are.
4. Do not overstay your welcome. You cannot monopolize any one person.
5. Depending on the response to you, get the business card.
6. Follow up!

"Yes, once you do your homework, you can target the room," La Mell says. "But, absolutely *never* ignore people. Each individual is a potential connection, and you have to treat everyone with regard."

Again, it's authentic interest and gracious manners that get the response.

La Mell's point is echoed by others: *"Make the connection and do not belabor your point. Following up in a social way is a soft sell and establishes rapport."*

HERE COME DA JUDGE

We must be very careful about our judgments. A colleague was on a San Francisco Opera committee with the "society" and "wanna-be society" people. "I am a lover of opera and happy to contribute my time and energy to supporting this art, but tolerating intolerance was *not* acceptable to me." Let's not be memorable for the wrong reasons! My colleague clearly remembers those whose snobbish ways were insulting. That is *not* how to "work" any room.

PARTY POLITICS

At a political fund-raiser, everyone has to donate money in order to attend. The reasons for donating money to a candidate are as varied as the number of people in attendance, but everyone has in common an interest in the candidate or the organization's success.

Often there is Big Name Entertainment . . . but the real "draw" is a chance to meet the candidate or officeholder. If the politician is working the room properly and you are not hanging out behind the curtains, *you should get that chance.* Make the most of it. Put yourself forward in a gracious way, introduce yourself and say something memorable—and brief. The politician wants to meet and connect with you, but he or she may need to do the same with hundreds of people in only a few hours. A short, unusual quip will make you stand out in the sea of faces.

We assume that all politicians have mastered the art of working a room. After all, the phrase "working a room" came to us from politics. But this isn't always the case. Politicians have all the same roadblocks we do. They, too, are 88 percent shy. It's just that their very survival depends on remedying those roadblocks. And they wouldn't be where they are if they hadn't had some success in doing so.

Can you imagine a politician who heeded Mother's Dire Warning: "Don't talk to strangers"? That's a politician who can barely pay for his meal, let alone buy television advertising! And how would you like to be one of that politician's constituents? Until you'd been properly introduced, you couldn't even tell him about the pothole on your street.

A former San Francisco mayoral candidate told me, "The fund-raiser in my honor was much easier because people who attended were supportive. The issue for me was balancing two to four conversations at once with people who wanted several words *alone* with me. I believed I owed each person that time and tried to do just that. And it was tough. The event that honors someone else is different. You have to judge the event and the

people and not overstep your bounds. It is poor campaign form to get up and move from table to table when
you are *not* the honoree. We need to exhibit manners and
respect for protocol and for other people."

His comments are instructive for us nonpoliticians as
well. If we table-hop to work someone else's room it may
backfire.

San Francisco mayor Willie Brown is a masterly mingler. What can we learn from this master of working a
room? Beyond the obvious charmers—eye contact, smiling, touching, shaking hands, humor, speaking and listening to each individual, laughing—there is a special
warmth and sense of caring, because *he looks like he is
having a fantastic time himself.* Connecting with people
didn't appear to be a chore for him; it appeared to be fun.

When we honestly enjoy other people's company, we
hardly have to think about how to work a room. All the
"right" things come naturally, because we *want* to make
people feel comfortable and cared for. They respond to
that, and to us.

ROANE'S REMINDERS

The cocktail party—social, business or fund-raiser—is a perfect opportunity to meet new friends and new contacts, to reconnect with familiar faces and to have a good time.

Bring:
- your business cards
- your smile
- your focus
- your sense of humor
- your wit, wisdom and interest in others
- conversation starters: lapel pins, ties, jewelry, hats (when appropriate)
- appropriate manners fit for the occasion

Observe:
- the layout of the room
- gifts of gab (and say something)
- the people, the groups, the flow

Lose:
- prejudgments
- snobbery
- self-focus

WORKING THE REUNION: REELING IN REALITY

If you doubt that reunions are a major cause of weight loss in America, just ask anyone who has ever attended one. My twentieth high school reunion in Chicago prompted three weeks of starvation and many questions.

Why would any busy person leave her business and home for days to reconnect with the past? Why would any sane person fly two thousand miles to see high school classmates? My motive for going was a combination of curiosity, friendship, business and lots of warm feelings for a very nice group of "kids."

It was worth every moment of fear and trepidation. I had a terrific time, reconnected with old friends. A pleasant and *unplanned* by-product of attending my most recent reunion with the "kids" was a number of speaking engagements with their companies. Go figure!

JUST GO!

At a reunion, the room is *not* filled with strangers! For some, this is a plus. You definitely have something in common with your old classmates—even if it's a dreaded algebra teacher of days gone by.

For others, having a history with these people is a drawback. The invitation to the reunion may unearth old pains and insecurities. (Who among us was truly secure and serene at age seventeen?) It may prompt fear about comparisons—professional, social, marital and monetary.

And always, always, there is the Pound Problem—for men as well as women. Gloria Steinem tells the story of her Smith reunion, and says that no one was as concerned about professional success, marital bliss, children or who had found the meaning of life as they were about WEIGHT. The first thing everyone said to her was, "You're so THIN!"

The thought of voluntarily returning to celebrate the days of yesteryear can be chilling! Will it be too disillusioning to see the football hero with a beer belly and a balding pate? Or to discover that cheerleaders have *thighs*? Don't let a few extra pounds or lost hairs stop you from saying yes to the reunion invite.

Will everyone want to probe your personal life, picking for imperfections? Will they want to see your last six bank statements? Hear all about your first date after the divorce?

Probably not.

The fact is, people are clamoring for reunions. One reason is that Baby Boomers are reaching the age for thirty- and forty-year reunions. And, Generation X has hit the ten-year reunion stage. Another reason is that, despite all the terrible trepidations and worst fears, despite the months of dieting and starvation and aerobics, despite the foreboding about seeing the person with whom you did "everything but" and despite the time and expense that is usually involved, most people have a fantastic time at their reunions and would do it again tomorrow!

The reunion is a formal social event with a long history, and it is more popular today than ever. The yearly family reunions are proliferating. People want to connect with family, friends and roots.

Across the country, people are overcoming the usual reunion neuroses—what to wear, what to weigh, what to

do, what to say—and are flocking to their reunions. Judy
Markey, a Chicago radio host and author of *How to Survive Your High School Reunion and Other Mid-Life Crises,*
recommends that we "abandon all that knee-jerk nega-
tivism, and just GO. Here's why. Because sullen, difficult
adolescents actually metamorphose into wonderful adults.
You'll be in a veritable roomful of you're-not-getting-
older-you're-getting-betters."

Besides, now that you know how to work a room,
you may come away with a whole new group of friends,
people whose presence is fresh and exciting but who also
knew you "when." Reconnecting is powerful—especially
when we don't have to fill in the beginning, and people
know us and our families.

Last but certainly not least, you may discover some
wonderful business contacts among your old gym or
geography buddies.

REUNION REFERRALS

My primary purpose in attending my reunion was to
reconnect with old friends and, frankly, to see what had
become of people since we last saw one another twenty
years ago.

Business opportunities aren't limited to your former
classmates. If you are traveling to your hometown, give
some thought to other potential contacts there. For me,
scheduling a book-signing, a presentation or an appointment with a Chicago-based corporation or association-
meeting planner was an added bonus.

I took business cards with me to the reunion. Even if

you only intend to socialize, it is far better to exchange cards than to write your address or phone number on a used napkin. It's important not to be consumed by the potential business aspects of a reunion or you risk creating the impression of a "hard sell," but reunions are an excellent opportunity to reconnect and interact—and people prefer to do business with people they know, like and trust. Now, with e-mail, we can offer our cards and stay connected for the cost of a local call!

Prepared to do business as well as to have a wonderful experience, I got both! Old friendships were renewed by talking about "the good old days," and were enhanced by the added dimension of talking about our business/work lives as well.

If you are interested in business as well as pleasure at your reunion:

- Plan ways to initiate contact and follow through.
- Contact people before the reunion to show your interest in them.
- Practice an upbeat, interesting, concise introduction that includes something about what you do for a living.
- Ask for leads, and *offer* leads.

I'm not suggesting that you set up a card table just inside the door with your name flashing in neon above it. Don't overwhelm people with your information; just let them know what you do—when it is appropriate. There is no point in offending people with an inappropriate "hard sell." Besides, *the first reason to attend any reunion is to "reunite" and have fun.*

PREPARING FOR THE REUNION: A WEEK TO LOSE TWENTY POUNDS

Start preparing for your reunion *early.* You'll want more than a week to tackle those twenty pounds, and more than a few hours the morning your plane leaves to get yourself ready—physically, psychologically and professionally. You'll work the room with ease and grace by preparing in advance:

ATTITUDE

Go with the idea of having fun, and don't fret about what people will think of you. Remember, the best way to overcome self-consciousness is to concentrate on making others feel comfortable. *No one* attends a reunion without some second thoughts.

Being genuinely interested in people should be no problem here. Who can resist wondering what has happened to the Prom Queen (now the mother of six), the Class President (now a jazz musician), the Serious Student (now a TV anchorwoman making six figures) or the Class Nerd (now a software genius who could buy and sell everyone in the room six times over, and has also developed a charming personality)?

A friend recently attended her twenty-fifth *grammar* school reunion, and found herself talking with the Class Nerd. This guy used to stand five feet three and weigh one hundred pounds dripping wet, but a quarter of a century later he was six feet two and gorgeous. She remarked on how people had changed and he replied, rocking back and forth on his heels, "They sure have. Me? I discovered testosterone. . . ."

Keep an open mind. A lot of nice things happen to people in ten, twenty, thirty years, and it is a good idea to give your old classmates a clean slate. Barry probably doesn't throw spitballs in board meetings the way he did in history class. Randy may have sworn off hurtful gossip nineteen years ago.

And remember, you have nothing to prove. Be yourself and enjoy.

NAME TAGS

Be sure to sneak a peek at the name tag just in case you don't recognize someone. Mercifully, some of us are late bloomers. You may want to glance at your yearbook before the event.

FOCUS

Identify the people to whom you definitely want to talk, but be open to serendipity. Allow for the unplanned and the unexpected. That could mean a business referral or a romance. You never know what you'll find out about your old friends or their interests.

During my visit to Chicago for my reunion, I went shopping at Marshall Fields—another reunion in itself! When the saleswoman heard why I was in town, she told me about her recent fortieth reunion. Two people, a widow and a widower, attended alone. Within ten months they were married and had moved to Miami! This was before South Beach was cool.

Who knows? You may even fix up your son with your classmate's daughter! Or your brother with a classmate's sister. Or recruit a classmate to work for your pre–IPO company.

One focus to avoid is proving to people how much you've changed, or worse, how successful you are. These tactics usually backfire, and aren't much fun anyway. The people who use them put themselves, and other people, on trial.

Concentrate on the pleasure of connecting with old friends in new ways . . . and don't worry if you've lost some hair or gained a few pounds in ten or twenty years. Most of us (certainly, those of us who have matured) know that it isn't the cover that counts, it's the contents.

CARDS

I'll say it again. Don't leave home without them. Not only do you avoid the wine-soaked napkin routine, but exchanging cards leads to follow-up correspondence and communication that renews friendships.

Build your Millionaire's Rolodex,™ even if all your contacts are purely social.

It's important to exercise good judgment and good taste when handing out your cards. One man at a reunion arrived late and moved through the banquet, dropping a handful of cards at each table. I doubt that he received any business from such a tacky tactic.

A family friend used these suggestions for her thirtieth reunion of Denver High School. "At my other reunions, I was fairly quiet. This time, I prepared, read, had some questions and conversation ready. I had nothing to lose so it was easier to approach classmates I recognized and those I didn't. It was a blast!"

See, it works.

REUNION TIPS

SPOUSES AND SIGNIFICANT OTHERS

Leave home without him! Experts on reunions almost universally agree that husbands should be left at home.

You will notice the use of male pronouns. This is gender-biased and for good reason. The scientific studies aren't in yet, but empirical evidence suggests that while the "boys'" wives manage to fit in and even, in some cases, have a good time, the "girls'" husbands *suffer visibly.*

Perhaps this is because they aren't used to their wives being the center of attention, perhaps because they aren't accustomed to being schlepped (see Glossary) to events as the "significant other," perhaps because the "boys" are fascinated to see the "girls" but could not care less about their husbands. Who knows? What is increasingly evident, however, is that to bring your husband or male significant other to a reunion is to invite disaster. It will definitely put a damper on your good time.

There are exceptions, but they are rare. Rick Enos, restaurateur, actually had fun at his wife's reunion because

"I never had to feel bad about forgetting a name or a face." Michael Hirsch, Mr. Chia Pet, brought his lovely lady friend, LuAnn, to his twentieth reunion. He observed how at ease she was with his friends and how much they liked her. "It was a huge wake-up call." They were married within the year!

David Peterson—then a significant other, now a spouse—had a terrific time at our reunion. Peterson, legislative director of the Chicago Teachers' Union, offered, "I go out with the intention of having fun. I basically enjoy people and I felt the joy you all were having at your reunion."

Peterson could make a fortune giving seminars for other males on "how to be spouses." "Bride" training for men?

HUMOR

Bring a healthy sense of humor. If you can laugh at whatever gaffes or goofs you make, people will be more comfortable with you.

No one liked being the butt of jokes or sarcastic remarks back in high school, and they are even less likely to enjoy it now. Perhaps Eddy didn't like being teased for "throwing like a girl" on the playground. Now that he owns a professional football team, he'll like it even less. And Debby got rid of her braces twenty years ago, so let's give her a break even though it was very funny when she kissed Arthur at the Junior Prom and they "got stuck." *She* can bring it up, but be careful and ready to back off if *you* do.

TALK TO EVERYONE

Our tastes and values have changed in one, two or four decades, and so have *we*. Other people have changed, too. Move around the room and speak to everyone. You never know what treasure you'll find. The nerd of yesterday could be the nice guy of today . . . and tomorrow. And there are cliques. One clique of our "girls" was known for being stuck up then, and they stuck together at our last reunion. But the other wonderful women and men of Mather High were delightful!

TIME TRAVEL TIP

If you travel "back home" for your family, high school or fraternity reunion, build in some time to reconnect with other old friends.

When I went back to Chicago, I planned separate get-togethers with my old college buddies. While there, I also took a deep breath, clenched my teeth and called my first college boyfriend, David Schultz, who is an attorney in Chicago. I had not seen or spoken to him in eighteen years. Nothing ventured, nothing gained. What I gained was a dear friend and staunch supporter.

FOLLOW UP

Reunions are a wonderful networking opportunity both for friends and for business associations—but only if you follow up. It doesn't matter how significant your connection over the punch bowl was. If you don't follow up, the opportunity is lost. E-mail and calls, notes, faxes are some of the many ways to stay in contact.

That's just as true for social connections as it is for business contacts.

Take a few minutes to write notes to the people with whom you had particularly pleasant experiences. Let them know, at the very least, that you enjoyed seeing them again. If you want to go a step farther and renew the relationship, suggest writing and/or getting together. And if you discussed business, by all means send them your brochure if they asked for it . . . and any other information you think they might find interesting.

PAYING OUR RESPECTS

There are some "reunions" we attend that have a serious, even a sad, purpose. Yet our presence is important and may speak volumes about who we are, our priorities and our respect for others. Attending a funeral, wake or life celebration service is never easy.

We often worry about what to say and sometimes don't attend because of that worry. I interviewed people in bereavement for *What Do I Say Next?* There were some who felt abandoned by friends who "disappeared" and others who were grateful for the support of friends, colleagues, coworkers and bosses.

What we say is not as important as our presence. A simple touch on the arm and an "I don't know what to say. My thoughts are with you" is comforting. Sometimes it's a story we have of the person that reflected their character, interests and humor. When we share the story, it gives the bereaved comfort.

Remember: Avoiding a hospital visit, memorial service or funeral because WE are concerned about OUR discomfort is unacceptable.

In our multicultural workplace and world there are varying customs. To feel more comfortable, ask your friends and coworkers for advice or call up www.askjeeves.com on the Internet.

Are these rooms "to work"? Absolutely NOT! But reuniting with an old friend or former coworker at a wake, when we are all paying our respects, can reconnect us in myriad ways.

ROANE'S REMINDERS

- Go to your reunion.
- Reunions are a chance to reunite with old friends and reestablish longtime connections.
- People have grown up, changed and are interesting.
- Have fun.
- Build your personal and business network.
- Connections with classmates can blossom into renewed friendship, romances and/or business.
- Prepare ahead of time as you would for other parties/events.
- Do your homework.
- Relax and enjoy yourself while you are there.
- Follow up.
- Connect with people as they are today.
- Start the diet and workout plan way ahead of time!
- Remember, anything can happen.

14

WORKING THE TRADE SHOW OR CONVENTION: THE TRADEOFFS

Trade shows and conventions are the Olympics—the supreme test of your ability to work a room. As they say about New York, if you can make it there, you'll make it anywhere.

Not only do trade shows and conventions feature almost *all* the types of events we've discussed—business meetings, "social" gatherings, cocktail parties, dinners, lunches, individual encounters and sometimes even reunions—but there are usually *hundreds* of these events, all crammed into the space of a few days to a week.

Some of the events on the schedule will be called "social," but make no mistake—this is business and requires the ability to work a room.

And it is work! Just ask anyone who has ever staffed a booth—standing! Or anyone who has walked through miles and miles of exhibits. Most women agree that the difficulty of these activities increases in direct proportion to the height of their heels.

But take heart. With a bit of planning and strategizing, trade shows and conventions can also be a tremendous amount of fun. After all, you are there to connect with people.

"Meeting your colleagues and friends is the most important aspect of a convention," said Tom Peters, author and management guru.

Whether you attend the trade show or convention as an exhibitor, a potential buyer, a representative of the facility where it is taking place, a member of the organization or simply as an interested party or the spouse of one of these people, certain strategies will help you get the most out of the event.

PREPARING FOR THE ONSLAUGHT

Most of us want to use our trade-show/convention time (and money) wisely. Getting what we came for is important not only to us, but to our employers. The folks who paid for us to be there expect success. And if we're self-employed and have shelled out the money for the conference, booth, materials, air fare and expenses ourselves, the event had *better* be profitable.

The time to start preparing is *not* when the plane touches down or when we get our first peek at the convention hall. First of all, it is easy to be overwhelmed by the sheer volume of things—the number of people to see, booths to visit, meetings to attend, parties to drop in on—and by the immense physical distances to be covered. It's not unusual to attend six to eight events in the course of a day—and that's before the evening cocktail parties, dinners, hospitality suites and late-night get-togethers.

As the saying goes, "If you don't know where you're going, you're likely to wind up somewhere else."

Regardless of your role at the event, preparation is crucial. It should start long before you get on the plane.

Conventions and trade shows require a three-pronged approach to planning:

1. planning for the office to run smoothly while you are away,
2. planning for the time spent at the event,
3. planning for follow-up.

DON'T LEAVE HOME WITHOUT . . .

TAKING CARE OF THE FOLKS BACK HOME

With all you'll have to do at the trade show or convention, you don't need to be worried about what's happening back home—whether your mail is being answered, whether someone remembered to cancel your dental appointment, whether your clients are getting everything they need, whether someone is feeding your cat (and children!).

Make a list of the things for which you are responsible at the office and at home. You may have to delegate some projects or trade off some tasks, reschedule appointments and train someone to handle your tasks and phones the way you want them handled. With today's wired and wireless options, staying in touch with the office is easy.

At home, your preparation may include lining up baby-sitters or house sitters, finding someone to care for your plants or pets, alerting your neighbors that you'll be gone, determining which bills need to be paid, canceling the paper delivery, getting someone to take in your mail and the R.S.V.P. for a party that takes place just after you return.

Making these preparations not only lets you leave in comfort and enjoy the convention, but ensures that you won't come back to an overwhelming mess.

THINKING AHEAD TO THE EVENT

You can eliminate a million distractions by anticipating your own needs at the convention—and the needs of others.

First, get the facts straight—the dates, place, times, locations and accommodations. Most groups send an advance schedule of events, and some include a map of the exhibits. If you can, plan your route through the convention hall in advance so that you can see the people you want to see without walking extra miles.

Be sure you understand the financial arrangements. Does your company prepay the costs? Is there an expense account for entertainment? Do you cover costs and present receipts for reimbursement? If you are self-employed, financial arrangements and allocations must be built into your business's budget.

Second, you need to understand exactly why you are attending this convention. Are you there to investigate the latest trends, developments or products? Are you being sent to gather data or information from the seminars or to land new accounts? Will you be expected to report back? How detailed will your reports need to be? Is this a crash course for *you* to increase your skill, knowledge and effectiveness? It is important that you make these determinations before you go.

Perhaps you are attending this conference simply to increase your contact base. Much of what is learned and accomplished at a convention may be done informally. Sometimes I've learned more chatting with a colleague or mentor over coffee than I would have by attending six seminars. We can always buy the tapes, but it's the casual conversation in the hallway that may be valuable.

Third, plan your clothing. What you take will be determined by the location of the convention and the time of year. Find out what the weather is likely to be. Check the schedule to see if you'll need clothing for a meeting, an afternoon barbecue, a pool party, two cocktail hours and a formal dinner on the same day.

Take clothes that are appropriate and comfortable. Shoes should be *especially* comfortable. You won't be able to work the show as effectively if you are hobbled by blisters or if your feet are screaming for a rest. You won't have as much fun, either.

And remember, this is business. See-through, backless and frontless dresses are not acceptable. Nor are jeans for an awards banquet, in most cases. Nor Speedos for the pool party.

Our final banquet at our National Speakers Association convention is a formal occasion. Several men did not wear tuxedos. One colleague said he felt conspicuous and uncomfortable. The next year he wore a tux.

Fourth, be aware of the culture, norms and expected behaviors of the industry, profession or company. A convention of the National Restaurant Association will have a different character than a trade show for preschool educational toys. Different types of people will be present, and different behaviors will be expected. Know the world you're about to "work."

Fifth, schedule your travel arrangements so that you have some time to relax and recover from jet lag before you "hit the floor." Don't plan to land at 2 P.M. and attend a 2:30 P.M. meeting. Why arrive harried and out of breath at the airport, the registration desk or the meeting when you could have a better time being gracious and serene?

Patricia Fripp, an international speaker who travels hundreds of thousands of miles a year, believes in Thorndike's Law: Performance that is rewarded tends to be repeated. "This works for management and self-management," she says. Fripp rewards herself for arriving early at the airport by calling her friends and chatting. That way, the extra time isn't wasted, it's enjoyed. "The one time I cut it too tightly, naturally, was the time I locked my keys in the car! Now I build in 'catastrophe time' for freeway accidents and long lines at airport security."

And while we're on the subject of travel, remember that unforeseen circumstances always occur. Suitcases, boxes of materials and airplanes often travel to different destinations. Henny Youngman told this story: Checking in for a flight to Des Moines, the seasoned traveler told the airline employee, "Please send this red suitcase to Omaha, the blue one to Newark, and the box to Miami."

"Sir," the surprised employee replied, "we can't do that."

"Why not? That's what you did last week!"

Funny . . . sort of. Unless you are the traveler in question. Take your luggage . . . Please! At least take a carry-on with one change of clothing and underwear, plus toiletries and important papers.

*Sixth,*remember the basics. Prepare a positive attitude. Know your focus—your purpose and goals for attending the convention or show. It helps to make a written plan. Work on your self-introduction and develop conversation starters appropriate to the event.

PLANNING TO FOLLOW UP

Bring everything you will need to record expenses, take notes or tape seminars, collect and organize business cards and gather follow-up information. Bring your laptop and business-card scanner.

And of course you will bring your own business cards and company brochures. Ruthe Hirsch of Day at the Bay found the industry trade shows a superb forum for booking business. "I was always prepared to work all day at our booth and to follow up at the hospitality suites later that day. It was exhausting, but it was worthwhile," claims Hirsch.

"Follow-up is critical," says Chris Carr, meeting manager of AAA, who plans three hundred and fifty meetings per year. "I just attended a trade show and spoke to thirty different companies about booking my conventions. Only *six* sent the follow-up material promised!"

Include yourself in your follow-up plans. Most people forget to plan for "Regroup and Recoup" time when they get home, but I have found this to be invaluable. Build in time to unpack, sort mail, do laundry and just spend some "down" time before launching back into the routine. You've been in a completely different world, operating at a high pitch, and both need and deserve a mini-vacation—even if it's only a morning or an afternoon. In this fast-paced, nanosecond world, time for regrouping rejuvenates.

THERE'S GOLD IN THEM THAR BOOTHS

The booths at conventions and trade shows are places of golden opportunities, whether you are a buyer or seller. The whole point of booths is to bring large numbers of buyers and sellers together for their mutual benefit.

Whether you are behind the booth or in front of it, the *real* work occurs before you leave your office. Again, planning is the key. "Organization, attention to details and the ability to see the overall picture are essential to the planning and preparation," claims a Bay Area event planner.

"Preplanning is essential," says Susan Friedmann, the Trade Show Coach. "Take the time to learn about the association so that conversation flows more readily. It's too easy to talk to other purveyors or long-term clients. The goal is to establish new relationships. Also, reinforce for the staff that we cannot prejudge other attendees and must exhibit manners and extend our social graces to everyone."

Walking around the convention requires concentration and persistence. Faced with so many choices and so many people to see, it's easy to tune out, talk to whomever is around and turn the show or convention into a continuous party rather than stay focused on the goals. Stay focused, and take short breaks if you need them.

But there is a catch. A marketing strategy must be planned before you attend. That plan must also include the tactics that will be used and the goals established in terms of numbers of prospects and qualified leads.

For attendees, the trade show is a chance to research, assess and qualify products and services. It is also an educational experience, an opportunity to learn the state of the art and a way to eliminate telephone tag because the exchange of information is instantaneous.

Being aware of the benefits helps us to work trade shows and conventions more effectively and expedite business from both sides of the booth.

WORKING THE BOOTH

Staff training is *paramount*. Your staff needs to be well-informed about the product or service they are selling, about the competition and about how to draw business to the booth.

When they only know about their product, and haven't bothered to research the attendees who are potential buyers, they lose sales.

Homework works. It produces good connections, satisfaction, sales and good feelings for everyone involved.

THE THREE E'S

The people behind the booths should also exhibit The Three E's—Energy, Enthusiasm and Electricity—according to Pam Massarsky, secretary of the Illinois Teachers Union, who has worked both sides of the booth.

Your staff should prepare interesting tidbits as conversation starters. Since everyone at the show or convention will have a name tag, your people might open with a question or comment about the company and/or its location. They should also prepare questions about the attendees' needs or the suppliers' products and services. And they should listen to the answers. A smile for each trade-show attendee is a good start.

"May I help you?" is *not* a good opener for the exhibitor. It gives the attendee a perfect chance to say, "No thanks, I'm just looking." That closes the discussion; anything the exhibitor says after that might be construed as a "hard sell." They might as well be discussing shirts in Macy's.

"May I help you?" should be asked only at candy stores—where the customers are pre-sold. If you walk into Fanny May's or See's, you're not looking for Whitman's Sampler. You're there to buy Fanny May's or See's, and the only choice is between Tipperary Bon Bons or Walnut Squares!

A firm handshake, a smile, warmth and a (practiced) upbeat self-introduction will make the initial contact easier and more effective.

Make sure you are facing the trade-show traffic. NEVER should booth staff have their back to the attendees. Nor should they be so engaged in conversation with each other that they inadvertently ignore attendees. I have seen this happen too many times and always address it in my trade-show programs.

BOOTH DESIGN

Booth design is also important. Your booth should be attractive and capture interest. A gimmick can be useful if it has mass appeal. I suggested that one of my clients serve designer coffee and lattes. They were thrilled, as they had time for conversation while making cappuccinos and building contacts and rapport.

Nancy Shina used an interesting tactic. She believes that many booths are designed to create barriers. "Because the table can make the solicitation process intimidating for the buyer, we moved the six-foot table to the side, removing the barrier. The result was that the flow into the booth increased."

The unusual and original always make a booth more interesting. Dick Shaff, general manager at San Francisco's Moscone Convention Center, says, "Because we want to convey the hospitality of San Francisco as *everyone's favorite city,* our exhibit is a forty-by-forty-feet living room with a pianist. The people who staff our booth are good communicators who are well-versed in a segment of our convention or trade-show services."

THE THREE S'S

Joe Jeff Goldblatt of Georgetown University and coauthor of *The Ultimate Guide to Sport Event and Management Marketing* says, "Trade shows and meetings are theater for which you must know the script, schedule and staging. The script is that body of information you must give and receive. The schedule refers to the timetable as well as the appointments set *prior* to the event. Staging is equally important; you must know when and where to move. An off-peak-hours visit to exhibits or an early arrival at a general session provide excellent opportunities to meet colleagues. People prefer to do business with reputable, qualified friends."

Walking (or Working) the Floor

When you go around to see other people's exhibits, you'll want to be at your best. Here are some tips for conserving energy so that you can sparkle while you mingle and converse.

- Map out your route before you begin so that you are sure to see that the people you must see.

- Don't try to do too much in one day and arrive at the last booth looking (and feeling) as if you've just run a marathon.

- Make a list of people you want to see and things you want to do and carry it with you.

- Carry a small notebook or your Palm Pilot (or PDA) with you to jot down information and ideas.

- Resist the temptation to take everyone's brochure, gift and hand-out. You could be schlepping an extra fifty pounds by the time you work your way around the room.

- Stick as closely as you can to your normal regimens for food and exercise.

If you are used to working out each day, you may begin to wilt if you don't incorporate this into your routine. Some conferences schedule early-morning runs to accommodate joggers—and they are also a good place to meet people. Many conference facilities have tennis courts, weight rooms and saunas on the premises. Be aware of what kinds of foods and eating schedules allow you to function best. If you need a big breakfast, have one. But if you are grumpy in the morning, it might be a good idea to order from room service. Take care of yourself. Honoring your own routine is very important.

"CONVENTION"AL CHARM

At trade shows and conventions, business isn't always conducted around the booth. The "social" aspects of these events are just as important. I put "social" in quotation marks because if you are at a trade show or convention, *you are working*. But that doesn't mean you can't enjoy yourself, meet new people, reconnect with those you know and extend yourself to everyone around you.

These events are made to order for increasing your base of contacts. Make an effort to sit with people you don't know at dinners and luncheons. Take the initiative and introduce yourself to the people at your table. Ask them to do the same, just as you might at your local professional-association dinner meeting.

The "social" parts of the trade show or convention can be just as much fun, and just as profitable, as working the convention floor.

TRADE-SHOW TEMPTATIONS: TRYSTING AND TIPPLING

There are a few social aspects of the trade show or convention that bear some warning.

The trade-show tryst is a touchy issue. Miscommunication can make for uncomfortable situations. Be conscious of the verbal and nonverbal messages you send. Be clear about what you want, and what you don't want. Your boss sent you in good faith to represent the organization. Will an "indiscretion" get back to him or her—or to the other people in the office? How would this be received? How would *you* be perceived? Yes, you have a personal life and are entitled to privacy. But at a conference you are still on company time. Maybe my mother's "convention"al wisdom has a place here: "May all your 'affairs' be catered."

Drinking is another delicate subject. Sloppy behavior is usually offensive, and can mean losing a client, or even a job. Know your limits. Women are not expected to "keep up with the guys" at cocktail hour. So don't. Looking like you're ravaged by a hangover the next morning won't impress anyone. One insurance company hired me to do a program because the sales staff misplaced the collection of business cards they accumulated during an exhibit. Too much fun and alcohol blurred their judgment.

Convention behavior requires alertness, an ability to listen and comprehend and the capacity to give out information selectively. If liquor impairs any of these three areas, you will be less effective.

My father had a rule: None of his salespeople could

drink before 6 P.M., and they had a two-drink limit. He, on the other hand, positioned himself at the bar by 10 A.M. with orange juice on the rocks. He bought screwdrivers for everyone, acting as the congenial host and listening carefully to what everyone said. By the end of the day, he had learned much information about the industry and about his competitors. By sticking to straight OJ, he controlled the information he gave out—and he never, in sixty years, caught a cold at a convention!

Let common sense be the rule of thumb. Attend the sessions, learn, make personal and professional contacts and secure clients. Take notes, buy tapes, visit the exhibit hall and analyze the products for your boss. *Then* decide what you want to do for relaxation.

That doesn't mean you can't have fun. You can. A convention is a *balance* of work and play. Don't be a stick-in-the-mud, but remember that conventions can easily turn into three-day office parties—and some office parties can come back to haunt you.

The balancing act here is to keep your sense of humor without losing your perspective.

SPOUSES: TIRED OF GETTING SCHLEPPED ALONG?

It's not easy to go to an event where you are identified only as someone's spouse. Unless you are blessed with an abundance of the Dynamic Duo—chutzpah and charm—and make it your business to *start* fascinating conversations that are of interest to you, they don't always happen.

At one time, most of the spouses at conventions were wives who did not work outside the home. All that has changed. Now over 55 percent of the spouses who attend conventions work outside the home.

Joyce Siegel, who has attended medical conventions and meetings for more than forty years, has observed this shift. "More and more, we saw on the name badges that the doctor is female and the spouse is male. And the programs offered to us have changed. Flower-arranging programs have been replaced by estate and tax planning and time management."

Spouses must know how to work a room, too, so that they feel their time has been invested wisely. A friendly spouse can help you and the client. Nick Coles of Dana Corporation said his wife, Jean, made a new friend at one of the spouse programs. Her new friend was the wife of a manufacturer he had tried to meet. And they did—over dinner with their friendly spouses!

But some spouses enjoy socializing more than others. What does *not* work is to bring (or be) a Sullen Spouse, one who doesn't really enjoy either mingling or the convention itself. These spouses can often support their husbands or wives best by staying home and doing the things they do enjoy.

A TRADE-SHOW TRIUMPH

I know from experience that unless you're famous, or infamous, getting a book published can be a challenge.

My friend Jean Miller, a former librarian, knew I was writing a book. When the American Library Association convention came to San Francisco, she suggested I attend because every publisher in the country, large or small, would be there. Although Jean had already visited the convention, she consented to go again with me.

When the day came, I had a virus. I felt awful and didn't want to go. The thought of getting dressed up, organizing my materials, driving to Moscone Center and walking through miles of exhibits seemed like torture. I couldn't imagine working up the energy to approach people, converse, establish rapport and *maybe* spark their interest in my book.

I told Jean I just couldn't do it. She was sympathetic, but reminded me that it was "quite an opportunity." MY OWN WORDS, come back to haunt me. I went.

As we walked through the exhibit area, a publishers' booth caught Jean's eye and she insisted that I speak to the person there. Annie Cohen and I chatted and made a connection. I gave her my proposal . . . that was thirteen years ago!

You are holding the revised result in your hands.

This story is about a trade-show triumph, but it's also about the value of spending time with people who support you and your goals. Jean not only pointed me in the right direction, quite literally, she coaxed me toward my goals even when I was not feeling well.

ROANE'S REMINDERS

The trade show or convention is a unique opportunity to increase your base of contacts, to buy and sell products and services and to have fun. Where else could you find so many rooms to work in one place at one time? This is the big time, the marathon, the ultimate challenge to those of us who value the ability to work a room.

To get the most out of it and keep from being overwhelmed, plan the following in advance:

- the smooth running of the office while you are away,
- your work at the convention itself,
- your follow-up.

Working a booth or an entire trade show is just like working a room—only more so! Rise to the challenge, seize the golden opportunity and have fun!

More trade-show tips:
- Read the brochure.
- Devise a plan.
- Arrange for appointments ahead of time.
- Invite clients and potential clients to visit your booth.
- Stick to your eating and exercise regimen.
- Attend sessions (it's a great way to get conversational tidbits).

15

HOW TO WORK THE "TECHNO TOY" ROOM

This chapter is *not* about the latest gizmos or gadgets in the electronic world. It is about how, when and where to use—and *not* use them—the etiquette that speaks volumes about our behavior.

It saddens me that the subject has to be covered, but the gross errors in judgment in using the technology make the issue one that must be addressed. It is another facet of how to work and *not* work a room.

In 1991 I wrote about cell phone abuse. It's almost a decade later and the horror stories have increased exponentially with the speed of light/sound/modems. Pagers, cell phones, PDAs (personal digital assistants) and laptops are now commonplace. Calendars are now kept on computers, so one has to have RAM to make appointments which, of course, are easily cut, pasted or deleted. I tried to schedule an interview meeting with a client/friend for my last book, *What Do I Say Next?* "Sorry it's taking so long; my computer has a glitch," he apologized. "Get a datebook and pencil and you'll never have a glitch!" said I.

We think that these electronic gadgets have made our lives easier and, in many ways, they have. But they are also making our lives more complicated because of the expectation we have of using these toys. Once we invest the money, we have to justify the cost. It reminds me of the two-hundred-dollar pair of shoes I bought in Las Vegas when I was there to be the keynote speaker for a convention. It was easy to rationalize because I don't gamble! It was a whim based on some information I had from a fashion maven that "designer shoes were a must for my St. John knits." I was told people who counted would "know" my shoes were "quality." Oh, they are pretty. (Nobody ever noticed them!) But to justify my purchase and my guilt, I wear them . . . but only about four times a year, because the fit is not perfect!

And that is a phrase to remember! Whether it's an expensive pair of shoes, the three-thousand-dollar speakers for surround sound in a two-bedroom condo or the pager that vibrates (or, heaven forbid . . . beeps) during a vital face-to-face meeting, we must ask ourselves: *"Is the 'fit' perfect for the occasion?"* Or will it cause perfect fits?

CALLS OF THE WILD

In *The Secrets of Savvy Networking* I wrote of a man's pager beeping during an intense scene in *Cobb,* a dramatic play. That was in 1991 and the "scene" has deteriorated. Too many people are ruining plays, meals, conversation, parties and meetings by being "on call" and disturbing the peace!

As bad as it is here, reports are that cell phone use and abuse is even more prevalent in other countries. Colleagues have told me of restaurants in Hong Kong and Australia where most diners ate and talked—on the phone.

ATTENTION-GETTING DEVICES

Living in Marin County (north of the Golden Gate Bridge) affords me the constant opportunity to laugh at the ironic and moronic situations of life. I constantly read and hear about the refreshing concepts, precepts and principles of Eastern cultures, like being "in the moment" and being "mindful." But now I hear these phrases roll off the lips of the people who profess to be "in the moment" and are wearing a pager—to be in the next moment! Give me a break.

PAGING ... ALL (SELF-IMPORTANT) PEOPLE

Pagers have a purpose and are important for business and for emergency messages, if our spouses/bosses/parents/children need to find us. What irritates the rest of the people in the room in which we may be working, eating, exercising or enjoying a family celebration is that it interrupts the moment. The implicit message is that we (and/or our project) are *not* important. So, how "mindful" of "being in the moment" is that?

It's not an age or gender issue. This is one that crosses all lines. Call me old-fashioned, but I would not insult people by being on call to others . . . when I am in a meeting, at a party or having dinner with someone.

My "baby" brother, Ira, is a very easygoing guy with a

wonderful sense of self and sense of humor. Even down-to-earth, mild-mannered "baby" brother Ira got caught in the pager predicament. He had been in business with our father, who had been in the paper business for over sixty years. So, when Ira went to the club to work out during the early morning or late afternoon, no gizmos were needed.

When the Nate the Great passed away, Ira, like millions of us, became a sole proprietor. So he started wearing a pager. When he was working out with his exercise partner one day, his pager went off. He looked at the number and saw it was from one of his wax paper suppliers and determined that the return call could wait till the next morning. "Julie, my workout partner, went nuts. She told me I was so rude not returning the call immediately. Her point: Why bother wearing a pager if you don't return the business call?"

"The way I see it is that I get to make the determination. If I had been in a meeting during work hours, I would not have stopped the meeting with other people to return the call.

"We created quite a community conversation in the health club by soliciting opinions of other exercisers. Come to think of it, we created quite a buzz and did get people talking with us and each other. That was a great by-product," Ira said. He laughed and continued, "Julie still won't admit I was right!"

"LOCK 'EM IN A CELL" PHONE!

While road rage is all the rage, cell phone outrage is hitting the national boiling point. It's even replaced call-waiting as a viable, visible and auditory violation! According to *USA Today*, cell phone users (as of June 1999) numbered 76.2 million people! That's a lot of battery life and potential abusers, and the abusers seem to outnumber the users. Everyone has a story of rude, inappropriate, thoughtless cell phonies. And, yet, there are lifesaving stories as well.

Judge Philip Vick of Denton, Texas, appeared on the *Today Show* because he hands out contempt-of-court fines to people whose cell phones ring in his court. One third were attorneys and two thirds were spectators. But when a witness's cell phone rang, Judge Vick had had it! (So have the rest of us!)

The abuse of cell phones has gotten so bad that it has become the top diner's complaint, according to Allan Ripp of the Zagat restaurant guides. In several New York restaurants, cell phone users are asked to leave the dining

"Eat your lunch, and then we'll see about giving your phone back."

room to use their phones. Union Square Cafe in New York City is one restaurant that directs (requests) cell phone users to go to the (pay) phone area.

People can lose business by *not* knowing how to "work" a techno toy in a room, especially if there is an important meeting in that room. Leigh Bohmfalk, director of marketing at an Internet start-up company, had to hire a new public relations firm who would get a thirty-five-thousand-dollar-per-month account. For the third meeting, she arranged for their vice president to meet her CEO. "Not three minutes into the meeting, Mr. PR's cell phone rang and he took the call! With that he lost an account worth almost half a million dollars a year!"

SELF-IMPORTANCE SYNDROME

Yes, people do answer their phones in the middle of movies, plays and operas. When we are paying for an evening's entertainment (add baby-sitting costs for a young couple), having someone talk on the phone is annoying. One Michigan movie chain (Star Theaters) prohibits cell phone use and has added a special trailer that says so. Even though the no-cell-phone, no-pager announcements are now made in movie theaters, some people ignore the request. Self-importance is at a national high!

In 1999 actor Laurence Fishburne stopped a Broadway performance of *Lion in Winter*, to ask a cell phone user to leave. This was met with enthusiastic applause. For an actor to get "out of character" is out of character. Mr. Fishburne must have been incensed.

Cell phone abuse is intrusive. A manager of a small boutique feels she "has no choice but to be included in someone's personal conversation when customers answer their phones in the boutique." And she doesn't *want* to be included. "Their conversations are none of my business."

HOUSE CALLS

As an aside, for decades, doctors who were "on call" managed to get to their patients, deliver babies, perform emergency surgeries and *not* have beepers, pagers and cell phones. They went to parties, restaurants, symphonies and other events and still could be "found." Amazing! Life—and life-threatening—situations went on before cell phones and pagers went off!

A retired pediatrician lamented that there were no cell phones back in the early days of his medical career. His wife, Ruth, said it would have made the practice of house calls to sick children so much easier. "What irony," Dr. Bill Silverman added, "now we have cell phones and pagers—but no one makes house calls!"

MASS IGNORANCE

Several years ago I attended a funeral mass for a teenager. In the middle of one of the prayers the unthinkable happened: Someone's cell phone rang. My heart sank! How could anyone be that self-absorbed, self-important and rude? The thought that washed over me was a prayer. I prayed that the parents and family of this young man did *not* hear that phone.

Maybe the person just forgot to turn off the phone. The reality is that phones and pagers do *not* belong with us in a religious sanctuary. Especially not at a funeral service. The techno toys have no place in these "rooms," which are sacrosanct. When we are caught transgressing the boundaries of good taste, the impression is both poor and indelible.

Of course, I thought it was a one-time techno transgression until I spoke in Dallas/Fort Worth, where I learned of a similar situation. "When a woman's cell phone rang in church, at a funeral service for a youngster we knew, I was annoyed and embarrassed and worried. She was sitting next to me and I did not want anyone to think it was my phone that rang!" lamented one of my clients.

Even Fox's Mad-TV satirized the intrusion of the cell phone in a funeral service, highlighting the inappropriate behavior of people who misuse them.

THE TECHNO TERRIBLE: "DIS"CONNECT CONFERENCE CALLING

I was giving a presentation for a major international training association of great renown and repute. The clients had to schedule conference calls to go over every detail. After one of these tedious calls, I excused myself and said good-bye. Then I tried to return another call, but when I picked up the phone to dial, there were voices. The two women were continuing the conversation, but had missed one technological detail: They had not disconnected "conference call." I stayed on the line and listened to the two women. Who would have thought that I would have heard their foolish, mean comments about the program? Had they mastered their technologically advanced conference call feature, I'd be out some great material, which I have shared with many mutual acquaintances, audiences and colleagues.

I chose not to confront them, but I know the opportunity will present itself for me to address this on my own terms. . . . Guess I just did!

SCHOOL DAZE: HOW *NOT* TO WORK A SCHOOLROOM

When you're a parent, the dos and don'ts of cell phones should be "apparent," but they are not. Sometimes the institution that teaches the children ends up teaching the parents. According to Terri Skov, "When lessons learned are for the parents as well, we really end up getting our money's worth."

The head of the school's *Weekly Newsletter* from Terri's sons' school recently had to advise parents to "turn off their cell phones when they are visiting classrooms or at school events." Apparently, several cell phones have rung during performances, during assemblies and during classroom visits. The metamessage: "You, my child, are not as important as the phone call from someone, or anyone, else."

As a former teacher, I can tell you it is disruptive. We used to admonish the disruptive student. The teachers of today get to educate the disruptive parent. The newsletter also reminded parents *not* to let their children bring their cell phones to school. Times they are a-changing.

SELF-IMPORTANT CELL PHONE QUIZ

Have you answered your cell phone:

1. In a movie or a play?   Yes ❑ No ❑
2. In a meeting?   Yes ❑ No ❑
3. During a business lunch with a client? Yes ❑ No ❑
4. On a date?   Yes ❑ No ❑
5. During a funeral service?   Yes ❑ No ❑
6. During a religious service?   Yes ❑ No ❑
7. a. At a wedding (yours)?   Yes ❑ No ❑
   b. At a wedding (someone else's)?   Yes ❑ No ❑
8. In a lecture hall?   Yes ❑ No ❑
9. In a restaurant?   Yes ❑ No ❑
10. At a party?   Yes ❑ No ❑

If you answered yes to any of these, please reread this chapter!

The most flattering behavior that occurs when the person says "Please hold my calls" is when we are in their office. To focus and pay attention to the person in the room . . . is respected, remembered and revered. And that is the sincerest form of flattery and makes a great impression.

COMMONSENSE CELL PHONE USE

There are some situations that make sense. An executive in Silicon Valley is also his sons' custodial parent. His sons check in with him via his cell phone. "It is the best way I can figure out to stay connected to them, no matter where they are and what they are doing, when I am at work—or out socially. My colleagues, staff, customers and friends understand that when I answer my cell phone, it's because I am Dad."

The caveat: If your kids call six times a day, your productivity could be at risk.

LOW-TECH NO TOYS

It's as simple as turning down, preferably turning OFF, the talk-radio station when a colleague, friend, coworker or family member is in the car. Unless it's the NBA championship game that you *both* want to hear, the message is, "You just are not important or interesting enough." And that is *no* way to work any "room."

PERMISSION VERSUS PRESUMPTION MARKETING

Fax machines are an older gizmo in the techno-toy room that are too often overworked. Seth Godin's book, *Permission Marketing,* should be mandatory reading for those who are not savvy networkers or smart marketers and misuse the fax machine as well as the World Wide

Web. Laura Fenamore, owner of Golden Gate International Speakers Bureau, Inc., has received twenty-page unsolicited faxes from speakers who want to work with her. "I don't know who they are and then my fax machine is tied up with promotional materials that I never agreed to review. Can you imagine the impression that makes on me? Why would I want to recommend to my clients a speaker with so little savvy?"

Red Dana of KQED, San Francisco's PBS station, echoes the sentiment. "People explore our website and add all the random addresses they can find to their lists. They then send out numerous e-mails (or faxes) about their products without seeing if there is a fit or picking up a phone and asking who the best contact would be.

"Someone sent me forty-two e-mails about their product! That was not a sign of persistence; it is purely presumptuous."

How we correctly use the gizmos and gadgets of the twenty-first century is determined by respect, regard and consideration of others. We just need to "play fair" in the techno-toy rooms we enter! And make sure we turn off those toys so that other people at the events, parties and meetings are not impacted by our use of them.

ROANE'S REMINDERS

Do
- Use your cell phone appropriately.
- Make sure your cell phone or pager has a vibrating option.
- Choose the least obtrusive ringer (forget the intro to the *William Tell Overture!*)
- Leave it in the car or office or at home when it is not appropriate to have it with you (see below).

Don't
- Take it to a church or synagogue.
- Take it to an important meeting.
- Take it to a funeral service.
- Take it to your child's school program.
- Take it on a date.
- Take it to a movie, play or opera.
- Take it on a job interview.
- Take it to a wedding or family celebration.
- Take it to a hospital room.
- Take it to a restaurant.
- Shout loudly to help transmit the sound. It doesn't help and it annoys the rest of us!

16

HOW TO
WORK THE
DIVERSE ROOM

In the twenty-first century, the variety of rooms we "work" will have a common thread: diversity. People in the room (be it for a convention, trade show, meeting, community gathering, bar mitzvah or company barbecue) will be different from us and from each other. Being comfortable with people who are diverse in myriad ways, and developing skills of conversation so that what we do and say are appropriate, are good manners and make good business sense.

After one of my presentations in Florida, a salesperson in the hospitality industry told me that moving from Washington, D.C., to Sarasota was a cultural shock. "In order to do business I was forced to develop my conversation skills, patience and memory! If I didn't ask about the daughter's soccer tournament or Grandma Rose's garden, doors were closed to me. I was not used to this kind of exchange, and had to slow down and become an interested listener in order to succeed in my new territory."

Some of the differences we will encounter are geographic; others are race, religion, country of origin, cultural, abilities/disabilities, interests, gender, preferences and the newest topic: age. The bonus of diversity: We get to learn from people who are different.

NEWSFLASH: The workplace has always held occupants of varying ages. And the young entering the workplace rooms have always had new and different skills and mind-sets. One reason the verbiage has increased is that there are more media venues looking for news items about age-related issues. Another is that the Baby Boomers, by our sheer numbers, are creating the generational conversations. And the young, aggressive, self-assured "free agents" confidently zigzag their careers, redefining loyalty and taking career risks unparalleled in prior generations in the workforce. This young group today is different in that they grew up more computer savvy than socially savvy.

BILL GATES'S SENIOR TEAM: GRAY MATTERS

Smart executives and managers are utilizing the experience of others. Mr. Gates has assembled a team of the experienced best and brightest to brainstorm for Microsoft. They range in age from fifty-two to sixty-two. He values their experience and relies on their knowledge and expertise.

Although age bias is prevalent, the "dotcom" companies are beginning to realize that management experience and skill are acquired over time, time that can turn hair gray, and are now searching for those seasoned executives.

Turnabout is fair play. GE's mentoring program has a

new twist: older executives have youngish mentors who are techno savvy (*The Wall Street Journal,* February 5, 2000). Theirs is a mutual respect for mentors of all ages.

The older and the young each have much to contribute to the equation. It boils down to Aretha Franklin's classic refrain, "R.E.S.P.E.C.T."—of people's skills, expertise and experience. We all need to be open to learning from different sources.

"HIRE AUTHORITY"

Because only the incompetent think they know everything, it's not embarrassing to admit a missing skill set. That's why I eat in restaurants. This book is being revised as it was written—using number two pencils with good erasers! Becky Gordon, who is skilled in using her computer and in her editing skills, is translating the hieroglyphics. (Don't e-mail me about my antiquated methods. I have heard it. Many people have looked at me pityingly for my lack of techiness.) Trust me, the method of draft-writing has no impact on book sales!

When my website went up over five years ago, in order to view it I had to hire a fifteen-year-old high school student to find it. And to teach me how to do the same. His skill and facility with the computer and the Internet were astounding. He taught me and I was grateful.

The free agent does what he or she does best and should be doing, and hires out the other tasks! That's why small-business owners have bookkeepers, accountants, graphic artists, attorneys and advisers. That's how our SOHO, free agent community survives and prevails.

BUILDING BRIDGES, BONDS AND BUSINESS
RELATIONSHIPS

Talking to different people is interesting but sometimes difficult. We shouldn't be patronizing or rude. There is the chance that the person in the room who is different from us could be our best contact.

The best advice is a gem from Sharon Gangitano, who researched American multicultural studies. Her advice, as an African-American woman, for conversing both professionally and personally with people of diverse backgrounds is simple.

> *"Talk to those different from you . . . as you would talk to those who are LIKE you!"*

We have more in common than not. Respect and focus on those commonalities and celebrate the differences. Most people have interests and talents, went to school, have parents or are parents, have kids and once were kids. We all want to be safe, have a nice roof over our heads, be free of financial worries and have our health. Some of us love the movies, others participate in sports, while others of us support the arts. Many people read books and have favorite authors. Others have favorite television shows. And most of us enjoy a good meal!

We have more in common than not. In the rooms where we work, as well as the rooms we visit for the conferences, meetings, board retreats or parties, we'll meet people with visible differences. We should not ignore them or avert our eyes.

LISTEN UP!

Some people will be different in nonvisible ways. Maybe it is English as a second language, accented by the first, or a case of carpal tunnel syndrome that makes a too-firm handshake painful. Or, maybe, a hearing loss that is not profound but is severe enough so as to make events with perpetual noise difficult. According to the National Academy on an Aging Society, nearly six million Americans have hearing loss.

If you are talking to someone at an event and you see them cupping their ear or notice a hearing device, take heed.

Tips for Talking to the Hearing-Impaired

- Face each person as you strike up a conversation.
- Enunciate but do not overpronounce.
- Add facial expressions.
- Don't cover your mouth or face with your hands.
- Listen patiently.

There are additional tips from Lisa Goldstein of the University of California Berkeley School of Journalism, printed in the *San Francisco Chronicle:* "Don't speak louder. Don't assume all hearing-impaired know sign language. Don't assume the person not responding is ignoring you. They may be deaf and ignoring you!"

I know at least twenty men who have either total loss of hearing in one ear or partial loss in both ears. Too many years of rock and roll and noise have taken their toll.

At business or social events, talk to the person on crutches or in a wheelchair. Since the car accident that caused her to become a quadriplegic, Lori Sneed, whose dad, John, and I met on a plane many years ago, has maintained and sharpened her wit. She has had to deal with the "curious." People will often talk more loudly to her. "I have told several waiters that I cannot walk, but that I hear perfectly well."

The Silicon Valley, Silicon Alley, Highway 128 and all other high-tech corridors are populated by smart teachers from many different countries. Jennifer Colton of Switzer Communications in Corte Madera, California, works with the high-tech and game companies. "The biggest mistake we can make is judging by looks! The guy in the jeans, with the pierced ear and nose and wearing Nikes, could be the founder of the company with lots of VC [venture capital] behind it!"

And those CEOs may speak in accented English, which requires us to listen more attentively. And to be patient. Go to an event in Silicon Valley and English is spoken with accents from Spain, China, Taiwan, England, Israel, Latin America and Japan, because our workplace is global and the rooms we work are diverse.

AGE GAUGE

Lana Teplick, a Boston-based CPA, observed the young techie from a client company who visited their office to help with a computer system. "He acted as if we were inept on purpose. Remember, we do all the accounting work for his computer company and would never expect the principals to know all tax code changes."

Her advice, so that "we can all get along" in the workplace, or in any room we "work" or walk into is, "Be patient. We all have different skills, a lot to learn from each other and we are trying our best."

And attitude is everything. We need to approach opportunities, challenges, "rooms" and people with interest and enthusiasm. Add to that ideas, words and stories that reflect "what's happening," and we have communication that counts.

REMEMBER: Patience is an antidote.

ROANE'S REMINDERS

- Be nice to everyone!
- We can be diverse in many ways.
- Celebrate our differences.
- Lose the judgments based on physical appearances or disabilities.
- Look for commonality.
- Talk to those who are different as you would to those who are the same.
- It is good business and good behavior to be open to all people.
- Lose the "some of my best friends" line. It is insulting, patronizing and not endearing.
- Focus on the event, which is the common factor.

We never know from where or when, the next job, client, tickets to the play-offs or friend will come!

17

WORKING THE WORLD: TRAINS AND BOATS AND PLANES

It's a fact of life: People who know how to work a room produce more results and have more fun.

You have the skills now, and may have started enjoying the benefits already. Why limit your ability to work a room to meetings, dinners, cocktail parties, business lunches and formal social engagements?

Why not make every situation you encounter a "room" and *work the world*? The worst that can happen is that you enjoy life more, and the chances are good that you'll also make new friends and improve your business. The casual conversation with a stranger could just "make your day" or theirs.

THE CORNUCOPIA OF CONTACTS

What is a room? Whatever you *make* it! It can be:

- the airplane

- the golf course
- the pool
- the bowling alley
- the bleachers at the ballpark
- the nightclub or theater
- the jogging track
- the supermarket
- the health club
- the department store
- the bike shop
- the sushi bar
- the video arcade
- the hardware store
- the bank
- the book store
- anywhere you go

You don't go to these places in order to work them, but as long as you have to stand in line at the supermarket, why not have a pleasant conversation? Will it bring you a business deal? Who knows? That's not the point. *The point is to extend yourself to people,* be open to whatever comes your way and, in the process, have a good time. One never knows!

Obviously, you have to exercise some caution. There are certain parts of town you probably don't want to work—especially at night. But what could it hurt to strike up a conversation with the man who works in the hardware store? You might just learn how to use that complicated VCR or the mail merge function that's been baffling you for two years or hear of a great restaurant that serves homemade food (isn't that an oxymoron?)!

PUBLIC SPEAKING

How we talk to people and treat them in public can be overheard and oft repeated. When we are curt, patronizing or rude to service people, others hear and that is a risk we should not take.

There is no reason to speak to the shoe-repair store owner, the copy center employee, the waitress or the latté maker unkindly. No matter how "rushed" we are, we have to take the time to be polite in those "rooms" where others "work." It could come back to haunt, like a "blaring witch"!

A friend who owns a speakers bureau told me she attended a party in the Napa Valley. She was chatting with a newly-retired couple who had just sold their dry cleaning establishment in Silicon Valley and they had many interesting stories about it.

Once they found out she owned a speakers bureau, they became very animated. "Two of our longtime customers are speakers. One couldn't have been nicer. The other was pompous and insulting. He would brag that he could 'buy and sell us' with his monthly income from two speeches." And then they told her his name.

As the world is a mini-mingling market, of course she knew him, and had attended a party where "he was drunk, loud, obnoxious and behaved inappropriately." This couple confirmed for her that his "party" behavior was *not* a one-time accident. "I could never recommend him to speak for one of my clients. Could I ever trust he knows how to behave? No way."

It behooves us to think before we speak! Santa and the rest of us are watching and listening!

THE PLANE TRUTH

Planes are great places to meet people. You have a captive audience. I met a significant person in my life on a plane from San Francisco to Los Angeles. Father Larry Lorenzoni and I spent an hour chatting, laughing, comparing publications and enjoying a meeting of the minds and spirits . . . on a higher plane, of course. What if I hadn't taken the risk and spoken to him?

But we do have to pay attention to verbal and non-verbal cues and honor people's need *not* to converse if that is their preference.

On a flight to New York, I sat with Rod Beckström, a very nice CEO of a Silicon Valley software company, who was on his way to a Wall Street soirée. We talked about some strategies to work the Wall Street event. He mingled . . . his former company merged and now he is CEO of Privada and one of the brains behind Brainticklers.

COMMON GROUND

What is unique about working the world is that there is always a clear common ground. Wherever you are, the people there with you are in the same situation.

If you are on the golf course, the common interest is golf. Keith Goto is an avid golfer from Honolulu, and most of the conversations he has with people he meets on courses across the United States center around golf. He rarely mentions his position as vice president of a *Fortune* 500 company. He lets his golf game speak for him. And since he usually shoots in the seventies, his score says a lot. *The Wall Street Journal* featured an article in which golf course etiquette, rituals and manners are being taught along with swings, putts and focus. The Executive Women Golf Association has chapters across the country because women are linking on the links in growing numbers. Golf is closing many gaps and gulfs.

If you are at the jogging track, the other people there will probably be joggers as well—or are thinking about becoming joggers. If you are at the ice cream store, everyone else will be just as interested in a cone, a scoop or a sundae as you are. You might even compare notes on flavors. On more than one occasion, we talked to other restaurant patrons about their orders and even shared desserts. What fun!

COUNTER INTELLIGENCE

Today's restaurants are now building in counter space for those who want to watch the food preparation. Casual conversations at the counters have led to business contacts and friendships.

The contacts you make while working the world may or may not evolve into friendships or business associations. You may never see these people again. Even if you don't, you've brightened your own day and someone else's with the encounter and have earned Planet Points!™

Sometimes these connections are profound, and sometimes they are fleeting but pleasant. When travel agency manager Lisa Miller was doing research on the best bike to buy, the manager of a local bike shop introduced her to another biker who also happened to operate a bakery.

A few weeks later, she needed a birthday cake for a friend. She decided to visit his shop, and he was behind the counter. "Ordinarily, I would have smiled, placed my order and left . . . *wishing* I had said something to him. But this time, I took a deep breath and reintroduced myself. He did remember meeting me in the bike shop. The reward for taking a risk: great service and a delicious, free cookie!" There are tasty rewards for taking risks!

THIS IS YOUR LIFE

Each of us has a similar story, an example of how circumstances and connections evolved into something wonderful. It doesn't happen by accident; it happens because we exert energy and take a risk.

It is said that "you can't give a smile away; it always comes back." The same is true of a kind word or a conversation starter. What goes around, comes around.

Seize the moment, wherever you are. Smile and say something—anything! Practice striking up conversations. As with everything else you practice, it will get easier and you'll get better at it.

The benefits are the best life has to offer—connections with other people. In a sense, "working the world" is just another way of saying "living life to the fullest."

According to adventurer and speaker David Smith (King of the Risk-Takers), the rewards go to the risk-takers. Those who are willing to put their egos on the line and reach out to other people create a richer, fuller life for themselves.

That is what this book has been about—reaching out, which it has for over a dozen years. It can bring you personal and professional success. Connecting with people, working the world, and your life, should bring you what you desire.

ROANE'S REMINDERS

- The world is a cornucopia of contacts.
- How we speak to people in public can be overheard.
- Four walls no longer define a room; it can be *anyplace.*
- Casual conversation can contribute to our base of contacts and business . . . and pleasure.
- Chance encounters can change our lives.
- Smile . . . say something!

18

THE GOSPEL ACCORDING TO ROANE: THE TEN COMMANDMENTS OF CONNECTING

I. THOU SHALT PREPARE

- attitude
- focus
- self-introduction
- conversation
- business cards
- a smile and a handshake

2. THOU SHALT ATTEND

R.S.V.P. and go! Act like a gracious host.

3. THOU SHALT TRY STRATEGIES

- Read name tags.
- Go with a buddy.
- Talk to "wallflowers."
- Approach and be approachable.
- Smile.
- Allow for serendipity.
- Listen.
- Care.
- Extricate courteously and circulate gracefully.
- Follow up.
- Call or send "thank-yous."

4. THOU SHALT SAY SOMETHING . . . ANYTHING

- Don't wait; initiate.
- Take the risk; the rewards are thine.
- Listen with interest to the response.
- Smile and make eye contact.
- Pay attention.

5. THOU SHALT MIND THY MANNERS

- Learn old and new etiquette and brush up on thy manners.
- Acknowledge others.
- Treat *everyone* nicely.

6. THOU SHALT AVOID THE COMMON CRUTCHES

- Don't arrive too late.
- Don't leave too early.
- Don't drink too much.
- Don't gorge at the buffet table.
- Don't misuse the buddy system by joining thyselves at thy hips.
- Don't bring thy cell phone.

7. THOU SHALT REMEMBER THE THREE E'S

- Make an EFFORT.
- Bring thine ENERGY.
- Exude ENTHUSIASM.

8. THOU SHALT DRESS APPROPRIATELY

Unsure? Ask!

9. THOU SHALT REMEMBER THE THREE C'S

- Courtesy
- Charm
- Chutzpah

10. THOU SHALT BRING THY SENSE OF HUMOR (NOT JOKES)

Use the AT&T Test™: Appropriate Timely & Tasteful

FOR THOSE
DESPERATELY SEEKING
SUSAN

A Speech Is Within Your Reach!

If you want to book best-selling author and in-demand keynote speaker Susan RoAne for your meeting retreat or convention:

"Work" my website: **www.susanroane.com**

Mail:	The RoAne Group
	320 Via Casitas, Suite 310
	Greenbrae, California 94904
Voicemail:	415/239-2224
Fax:	415/461-6172
E-mail:	Susan@SusanRoAne.com
For books and audio books	Your local bookstore or online bookstore or www.bookpassage.com

How to Work a Room

The Secrets of Savvy Networking

What Do I Say Next?

To "Ask the Mingling Maven" or for free chapters of my other bestsellers or for pickmybrainconsulting.com: the "Write" Coach . . . visit www.susanroane.com.

SOME OF SUSAN'S CLIENTS

CORPORATIONS

American Software Users Group
Anheuser-Busch
Apple Computer
AT&T
AutoDesk
Cartier Jewelers
Century 21
Equity Residential Properties
Hershey Foods
Lockheed Martin
Lucent Technologies
National Fire Academy
Procter & Gamble
SmithKline Beecham

ASSOCIATIONS

American Automobile Association
American Bankers Association
American Payroll Association
International Council of Shopping Centers
National Association of Realtors
National Football League
National Restaurant Association

ACADEMIC

Harvard University Alumni Association
University of Chicago Business School
University of Hawaii
Wharton School of Business

FINANCE

Andersen Consulting
Arthur Andersen
Chase Manhattan
Citibank
Managed Futures Association
Pennsylvania State Bank
Scudder Kemper
Transamerica Asset Management

MEETINGS INDUSTRY

American Society of Association Executives
Meeting Professionals International
Professional Conference Management Association
(PCMA)
Young Presidents' Organization (YPO)

YIDDISH GLOSSARY

The following are some of the Yiddish terms I've used in this book, plus others that you may have heard, know and find useful and/or amusing. I thought you would enjoy these definitions as modified from Leo Rosten's *The Joys of Yiddish*. I've added some expressions that are "Yinglish."

Bris   "The covenant"; a ritual circumcision ceremony observed on a boy's eighth day of life.

("At Ari Tandler's bris even I got squeamish when the mohel picked up the instruments.")

Bupkes   Insultingly disproportionate remunerations to expectations and/or efforts (said with scorn, sarcasm or indignation).

("Can you believe this Fortune 100 company wanted me to coach their executives for bupkes?")

Chutzpah Classic usage: gall, brazenness, nerve. ("It takes a dose of *chutzpah* to initiate conversations." RoAne's usage: courage, gutsiness.

("The crook embezzles from the company and then requests a farewell party! That's chutzpah!*")*

Cyberdreck Trash, junk, that of inferior quality; a vulgar term not to use around my mother—nor yours.

("When The Wall Street Journal *has described some of what is available in cyberspace as* cyberdreck, *it must really be awful!")*

Fe! or Feh! An exclamatory expression of disgust and distaste.

("They are serving pasta with scallops and kumquats? Feh! *")*

Kibbitz To joke, fool around; to socialize aimlessly.

("The group in the corner of the room was kibbitzing *over coffee.")*

Klutz A clod; a graceless person.

("Run a marathon? I am such a klutz *I'm lucky if I can walk off a curb without spraining my ankle.")*

Kosher Fit to eat; ritually clean, trustworthy, proper, ethical.

("Using e-mail to fire a person is NOT kosher. *[Neither is bacon, shrimp nor lobster.])*

Kvell   To beam with immense pride and pleasure.

             (*"The happy parents were* kvelling *at their son's bar mitzvah."*)

Kvetch   To fuss, gripe, complain; the person who does that.

             (*"Brenda is constantly* kvetching *about everything."*)

Maven   An expert; a knowledgeable person.

             (*"With the explosive use of cell phones, the manners* mavens *have their work cut out for them."*)

Mazel tov!   Good luck; congratulations.

             (*"I am so pleased that you were promoted.* Mazel tov! *"*)

Megillah   Anything long, complicated, boring.

             (*"Tell me the results of the negotiations. I don't want to hear the whole* megillah. *"*)

Mensch   An honorable person of integrity; someone of noble character with a sense of sweetness as well as of what is right and responsible. To call someone a *mensch* reflects deep respect.

             (*"Mark Chimsky, my dear friend and adviser, is a real* mensch! *"*)

Mohel   The person who circumsizes the eight-day-old Jewish baby in the ritual *bris*.

(The mohel *is regarded as a technician [and better be a darn good one] and is the butt of many borscht belt comedian's jokes, yes, including the one about collecting tips instead of fees.)*

Nosh

To eat between meals; a snack, a small portion, a nibble.

("Cousin Shelly prefers to nosh *and nibble than to eat three meals.")*

Nudge

To pester, nag; to give a surreptitious reminder of a job to be done; the person who is a nag.

("He kept nudging *her to stop smoking.")*

Oy vey!

A lament, a protest or a cry of delight. It expresses anguish, joy, pain, revulsion, regret, relief.

*("*Oy vey! *It is such a tragedy to lose a home in a fire. Thank heaven the family is safe.")*

Schlep

To drag, pull or lag behind. Someone who looks bedraggled and *schleppish.*

("Don't schlep *all those packages, you'll hurt your back.")*

Schmooze

Friendly and gossipy; prolonged conversation; act of chatting *with* someone.

("Ira and Michael schmoozed *for an hour at the party.") (Incorrect: "Ira* schmoozed *Michael at the party.")*

Schnorrer   A cheapskate; a chiseler.

("Talk about timing, that schnorrer, *Lisa, always manages to be in the rest room when the bill arrives.")*

Shivah   The seven solemn days of mourning for the dead when Jews "sit *shivah*" in the home of the deceased.

("During my father's shivah, *relatives, friends and his business associates from his sixty-four years in the paper industry came to pay their respects.")*

Shtick   A studied, contrived piece of "business" employed by an actor (or salesperson); a trick; a devious trick.

("Watch him use the same shtick *on this new client.")*

Shvitz   To sweat; steam bath where one goes to sweat (off a few pounds).

(When describing a very humid summer day in New York that made her sweat, Katie Couric said it was a favorite word to say [rather than do].)

Tumult   Noise; commotion.

("The noise level was so high that the tumult *interfered with conversation.")*

Tush	Derrière (a cute term); bottomed out.
	(*"One cannot work a room on one's tush."*)
Yenta	*Classic definition:* A gossipy woman who does not keep a secret. It may also refer to a man who does the same. *Newer usage:* Since *Fiddler on the Roof,* a matchmaker.
	(*"I do expect that in the next production of* Fiddler, *Yenta will sing 'Networker, Networker . . . make me a match.'"*)

POPULAR YIDDISHKEIT EXPRESSIONS: RHETORICAL QUESTIONS (RQ) YOU SHOULD NOT ATTEMPT TO ANSWER

- What am I? Chopped liver? (RQ)
- I need this like I need a hole in the head!
- Enough already!
- For this, I sent you to college? (RQ)
- It should only happen!
- Who needs this aggravation? (RQ)
- He knows from nothing.
- From that he makes a living? (RQ)
- You should pardon the expression.
- Wear (drive, enjoy) it in good health.
- You should live to be 120!

FREQUENTLY ASKED QUESTIONS (FAQS)

Here are a dozen questions I have been asked frequently over the last dozen years.

1. HOW DO I APPROACH PEOPLE?

Go to the person standing alone or to a group of three or more. Smile. Comment on the situation in common.

2. HOW DO I REMEMBER NAMES?

Focus on the person instead of your to-do list. Listen to the pronunciation. Repeat the name. Look at the person and read the name tag.

3. HOW DO I BECOME MEMORABLE?

Be:
- Energetic
- An interested listener
- Inclusive

- Engaging

Tell:
- Good, true stories

Have fun.

Be lighthearted.

4.   HOW DO I INCREASE MY SELF-CONFIDENCE?

Be prepared. Read the paper . . . and *People* magazine. Have three to five stories, news bits and questions prepared. Practice stories and casual conversations. Talk to people at the health club, in the checkout line, in line at the refreshment stand.

5.   HOW DO I OVERCOME SHYNESS?

Know eighty-eight percent of us feel we are shy.
Decide to work through shyness.
Observe the behavior and manner of an outgoing person you admire.
Emulate that person.
Take an acting and/or improvisation class.
Join a book club or discussion group or an organization in your area of interest (see question number 4).

6.   HOW DO I BREAK INTO A GROUP?

Choose a *lively* group of three or four people. Stand on the periphery. When acknowledged verbally or by eye contact, step into the group. Comment about the conversation. Do not segue to your own agenda.

7. HOW DO I GET OUT OF A CONVERSATION?

Gracefully. Shake hands, summarize the conversation ("It was fun [informative]. Glad we had a chance to meet [talk]."). Move one quarter to one third of the room away to another person or group.

8. HOW CAN I TELL IF THE OTHER PERSON WANTS TO MOVE ON?

Observe facial expressions and body language and listen for verbal clues. If you make it easier for the other person to move on . . . you will be remembered well.

9. HOW CAN I GET PEOPLE ON MY AGENDA?

They may have no interest in moving our agendas forward. That is not why they showed up at the event. We can only get people into conversation. The ongoing conversation, over time, allows for shared agendas.

10. HOW CAN I MAKE A BUSINESS CONTACT WITHOUT APPEARING TO COME ON TO A PERSON OF THE OPPOSITE SEX?

Be friendly, open. Dress appropriately. Shake hands; no other touch is proper. Monitor language—no off-color comments, swear words or double entendres. No sidelong glances; avoid the once-over.

11. HOW DO I MOVE FROM SMALL TALK TO BUSINESS?

Carefully. Small talk is the *most important* talk as it is how we learn about people and their interests. "Big" talk is earned . . . over time. Listen for a cue to segue.

12. HOW DO I "BREAK THE ICE"?

"Melting" the ice is a great skill of masterly minglers. The comments and questions relate to the event, venue, sponsoring organization. Start with a big smile and eye contact, which makes you "approachable" in any room.

REFERENCES

Babcock, Judy. "Etiquette, Manners; Boor No More." *Success* (June 1984), 42–43.

Baldrige, Letitia. *Amy Vanderbilt's Everyday Etiquette.* New York: Bantam, 1981.

————.*Letitia Baldrige's Complete Guide to Executive Manners.* New York: Rawson Associates, 1985.

Butler, Pamela E. *Talking to Yourself.* San Francisco: Harper & Row, 1981.

Givens, David. "The Animal Art of Getting Along." *Success* (April 1985).

Goleman, Daniel. "People Can Often Judge How They Impress Others." *The New York Times* (June 30, 1987), 14.

————."Social Anxiety: New Focus Leads to Insight and Therapy." *The New York Times* (December 18, 1984), C-1.

Jaffe, Elliot. "Getting Chutzpah." *Savvy* (November 1982), 34–38.

Keyfitz, Nathan. "The Baby Boom Meets the Computer Revolution." *American Demographics* (May 1984), 23–25, 45–46.

Korda, Michael. "Small Talk." *Signature* (September 1986), 78.

Markey, Judy. *How to Survive Your High School Reunion and Other Mid-Life Crises.* Chicago: Contemporary Books, 1984.

Minninger, Joan. *Total Recall: How to Boost Your Memory Power.* New York: Pocket Books, 1984.

Morris, James. *The Art of Conversation.* New York: Cornerstone Library, 1976.

RoAne, Susan. *The Secrets of Savvy Networking.* New York: Warner Books, 1993.

————. *What Do I Say Next?* New York: Warner Books, 1997.

Rosten, Leo. *The Joys of Yiddish.* New York: Washington Square Press, 1968.

Schwartz, David J. *The Magic of Thinking Big.* New York: Cornerstone Library, 1986.

637 of the Best Things Anybody Ever Said, collected and arranged by Robert Byrne. New York: Fawcett Crest, 1981.

Tannen, Deborah. *That's Not What I Meant.* New York: Washington Square Press, 1968.

Zimbardo, Phillip. *Shyness: What It Is, What to Do About It.* New York: Addison Wesley, 1977.

ROANE'S
RECOMMENDED
READING LIST

Allesandra, Tony. *Charisma.* New York: Warner Books, 1998.

Carducci, Bernardo. *Shyness: A Bold Approach.* New York: HarperCollins, 1999.

Ciardini, Robert B. *Influence: The New Psychology of Modern Persuasion.* New York: Quill, 1984.

Chan-Herur, K.C. *Communicating With Customers Around the World.* San Francisco: So Monde International Publishing Company, 1994.

Friedmann, Susan. *Exhibiting at Tradeshows.* Los Altos, California: Crisp Publications, 1992.

Goleman, Daniel. *Emotional Intelligence.* New York: Bantam Books, 1995.

Kawasaki, Guy. *Rules for Revolutionaries.* New York: HarperCollins, 1998.

Nierenberg, Gerard. *How to Read a Person Like a Book.* New York: Barnes and Noble, 1993.

Scheele, Adele. *Skills for Success.* New York: Ballantine, 1999.